CONFESSIONS
— *of a* —
CASTING
DIRECTOR

CONFESSIONS

of a

CASTING DIRECTOR

HELP ACTORS LAND ANY ROLE WITH
SECRETS FROM INSIDE THE AUDITION ROOM

JEN RUDIN

itbooks

AN IMPRINT OF HARPERCOLLINS PUBLISHERS

*it***books**

CONFESSIONS OF A CASTING DIRECTOR. Copyright
© 2014 by Jen Rudin. All rights reserved. Printed in
the United States of America. No part of this book
may be used or reproduced in any manner whatsoever
without written permission except in the case of brief
quotations embodied in critical articles and reviews. For
information address HarperCollins Publishers, 10 East
53rd Street, New York, NY 10022.

HarperCollins books may be purchased for educational,
business, or sales promotional use. For information
please e-mail the Special Markets Department at
SPsales@harpercollins.com.

All photographs courtesy of the author except where
noted. Casting breakdown on page 30 used with
permission of Breakdown Services Ltd.

FIRST EDITION

Designed by Janet M. Evans

Library of Congress Cataloging-in-Publication Data has
been applied for.

ISBN 978-0-06-229209-4

14 15 16 17 18   OV/RRD   10 9 8 7 6 5 4 3 2 1

For my parents, Marcia Rudin and Rabbi James Rudin. Thank you for supporting my creative passions, schlepping me to all my auditions, and assuring me I was talented even when I didn't get the role. Mother, I won't forget to let you swim in my pool when I become rich and famous.

For my sister, Rabbi Eve Rudin. You are the best sister in the world and a constant voice of rational wisdom. Thank you for costarring in all of our childhood productions when I know you really wanted to be watching *The Bionic Woman* instead.

For Emma Mollie Weiner, my supercool niece. It's clear from your always original Passover plays and love of singing that you've taken after your Auntie Jen. However, I would also be very happy if you decided to become a medical engineer or a rabbi like your mother and Grandpa Jim.

For Rabbi Elliott Kleinman. Thank you for encouraging me to read my book drafts out loud, and also for loving my sister.

And finally, for Andy Finkelstein. You encouraged me to bring the book to life and I am eternally thankful for your support. I love our life together and could not imagine a single day without you. Namaste, baby.

Without wonder and insight, acting is just a business. With it, it becomes creation.

—BETTE DAVIS

Contents

Foreword

If only Jen Rudin had asked me to write a simple blurb for her book, we wouldn't be sitting here at Le Pain Quotidien thirty-four days later.

For the last five weeks I have tried to prioritize, integrate, and concentrate effort in the service of effective goal execution: namely, writing this foreword. A blurb I could have banged out 48,960 minutes ago. Concise laudatory sentences are in my line. Write. Rewrite. Add. Edit. Stop. Instead, I've started and restarted versions of a foreword that in no way resemble what you see now.

The circumstances demand an explanation. What? Why? How could this have taken me so long?

Well . . .

Here's the problem. Sifting through the necro-bag of disfavored auditions is upsetting. So many disappointments. Some of my losses are my fault. Some are not. All the rejection twenty-two years in SAG-AFTRA can offer. It's bleak. Like *Ethan Frome*.

Would things have been different if I'd had Jen's book? Absolutely, unequivocally: yes.

When luck found me in 1992, I had no training and very little acting experience. I just happened to meet Ben Stiller at a deli. A more enterprising person would have wanted to learn everything they didn't know about acting, but enterprising would have interfered with my drinking. (I used to be a hoarder of alcohol, but I've given that up. Now I go to bead stores. I'm crafty.)

Focus, Janeane, focus.

Compose a foreword that is filled with: Insight. Information. Advice.

So many roles. There are so many acting roles out there that don't have to be played by white people, men, young kids, or girls with "high erotic appeal." (*Low erotic appeal* is a phrase once used by a director to tell me why I couldn't audition for a part where the appeal—erotic or otherwise— was irrelevant. But I liked the sound of it and I put it on my résumé.)

Now I'm not going to sugarcoat it—acting is tough. So many possibilities go unexplored. So many performances unrealized. Tapes unsent, unseen. Landing that first role seems near impossible when you're new to the game, and it all starts with the hardest part: the audition.

I've had plenty of audition fails in my life—my most epic fail was for the movie *Mona Lisa Smile*. The audition was once described as "the worst audition she's ever seen." She = the casting director. I hope she's okay. The Spanish Armada was "the worst naval disaster ever seen," and it took Spain ten years to recover. Le Pain, Le Pain Quotidien!

My least favorite auditions are the ones that never happened. Careers pivot on access to opportunity. Frustration comes when diversity in gender, age, ethnicity, and aesthetics are seen as liabilities rather than assets. This is unfortunately a very real part of this business, and it takes a strong person to survive the inevitable rejections.

My favorite auditions? All of them, the ones that *did* happen. Even when they sucked. I enjoy auditioning. I take it seriously. It's a chance to perform. Learn something. Meet people. Sadly, most scripts are not written by the Coen brothers. This means you will be polishing a few turds. It's important to get good at that because the better you are, the less turds you'll have to polish.

The epically awesome audition story? My hero, director Scott Elliott, cast me in a play called *Russian Transport* by Erica Scheffer. I loved being a part of the New Group Theater, and this was the role that got me my Actors Equity Card.

Remember, through all the auditions, the good and the not so good: Jen Rudin is on your side. Most casting people are. Casting directors want you to do well, and Jen is one of the best out there. She cast me in roles as varied as the voice of a giraffe in an animated movie and a federal agent looking for Nikola Tesla's lost designs.

My advice to you? Take Jen's expertise, knowledge, and skill set, and combine them with yours. Absorb the information until it becomes habitual, reflexive. Do everything in your power to optimize your chances for success, because it's a large school of fish out there, and they all want to be caught. Regrettably, show business is not a meritocracy. Act like it is. (If you want a meritocracy, check out the 2016 Olympics in Brazil.)

And so, dear reader, the choice is yours. Read this book. Learn it. Utilize it. *Or* become a common turd polisher. Trust me, you need this book. It'll make things a hell of a lot easier!

"Don't be afraid of it. It's just brunch." —Iron Chef Bobby Flay.

Now comes my French exit.

—JANEANE GAROFALO

CONFESSIONS

— of a —

CASTING
DIRECTOR

INTRODUCTION

THE CAT IN THE HAT SELLS BOLOGNA ON SESAME STREET

I n 1978, I was six years old, and my older sister Eve and I were obsessed with the television show *The Brady Bunch*. The show ran in syndication every night at six and then again at seven. *The Brady Bunch* dominated our daily lives so much that our family had to rush through dinner at six thirty to make sure we'd finish in time for the next episode.

By age six, I was already a budding young actress overflowing with confidence and certain that I was the perfect girl to play the role of Cindy Brady, should they ever need to recast. Cindy and I were both younger sisters with blue eyes and blond hair. And we wore hair ribbons made of colored yarn in our pigtails. Desperate to play Cindy, I mailed my first-grade class photo to the local station that aired *The Brady Bunch*. In my typewritten submission letter, I asked them to please contact me for an audition should the role of Cindy become available. At some point, my parents broke the news that the *Brady Bunch* episodes were actually reruns and not taped live. I quickly redirected my obsession to Melissa Gilbert, on *Little House on the Prairie*, and the Broadway musical *Annie*.

My parents were very supportive of Eve's and my artistic pursuits, which included weekly ballet classes. One day our Russian ballet teacher pulled my mother aside and said, "If I could combine Eve's body with Jenny's confidence and poise, I might have a ballerina. But I don't." So we quit ballet and I started acting classes at the prestigious Neighborhood Playhouse in

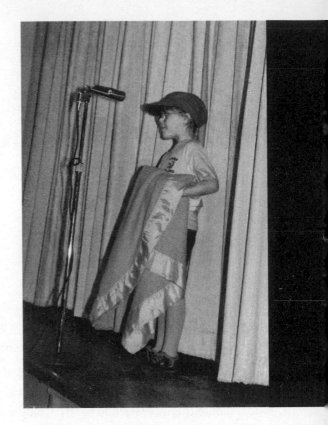

My photographic memory kicked in during rehearsals, and I could recite the script by heart. I mouthed everyone's lines during the performance while wrapping myself inside Linus's blanket.

New York City. Eve took up violin and music theory at the Mannes School of Music and started playing Vivaldi. I starred as Linus in our Hebrew school's second-grade production of *Charlie Brown Discovers Chanukah*, and met my first talent agent at age eight. I loved being onstage; I was hooked.

We lived on the Upper East Side of Manhattan, so it was easy for my mother to take me to auditions after school. I daydreamed of starring in my own TV series about a tomboy detective—Harriet the Spy meets Nancy Drew. I yearned to grace the cover of *People* magazine, like Aileen Quinn when she starred in the movie version of *Annie*. One small glitch in my road to stardom: I didn't love the audition process. Each audition held so much promise and possibility, but I was often met with rejection. Though my parents always told me I was talented, even when I didn't get the part, I lacked the ability to fully let go of the disappointment and took each rejection personally. I preferred to collect theater *Playbill*s and pretend to be a theater producer, setting up an office in our living room. I also wrote my own original scripts and short stories. I devoured Frank Rich's and John Simon's theater reviews in the *New York Times* and *New York* magazine. My photographic memory made it easy to memorize which actor was replacing another in a current Broadway show. And little did I know, but a great memory would really come in handy when meeting the hundreds of actors I would audition in the future as a casting director.

JENNIFER RUDIN

My headshots over the years: 1984 (SUZANNAH GOLD)

JENNIFER RUDIN

JENNIFER RUDIN

1987 (GLENN JUSSEN, jussenstudio.com)   *1988* (GLENN JUSSEN)

Epiphany #1: Getting Cast in an Afterschool Special

At age twelve, I had my first casting director epiphany at a final callback for an ABC Afterschool Special. The premise involved a group of five kids who lived in the same apartment building and often got into various forms of mischief. The casting breakdown* listed all the available roles in the movie, including a cute boy, a chubby boy, a trendy girl, a token ethnic girl, and a smart, sarcastic girl—the role I was up for. Over the years, I'd gotten feedback from casting directors that I possessed natural comic timing, so I always auditioned for the funny friend roles and rarely for the "dark and moody" girl. The one exception was in sixth grade, when I was cast to play a girl who died of typhus in a workshop production of a play about the Terezin ghetto during World War II. After my big death scene in Act II, one of the older actors carried my body offstage. I was out of my obvious

---

* A *breakdown* is the casting notice that a casting office (or other entity seeking talent) releases to agents through a company called Breakdown Services. The breakdown lists and describes all the open roles available.

JENNIFER RUDIN

Jennifer Rudin

1988 (GLENN JUSSEN)

1995 (GLENN JUSSEN)

comfort zone with this darker role, plus I had a major crush on the actor. After every performance, the director politely told me to "try not to smile" when I was being carried offstage.

It was the summer of 1985. I'd made it to the final round of auditions, and the director and ABC executives were choosing between two groups of kids. I'd had so many auditions for this particular television

Jennifer Rudin

1995 (GLENN JUSSEN)

My parents and I on our way to my first summer at Stagedoor Manor, 1982. I never played tennis. Sports were hardly the emphasis!

movie that I was practically commuting to the city on the Short Line bus from my fourth summer at my beloved Stagedoor Manor Performing Arts Training Center* in the Catskills.

I peered at the casting director from behind my signature thick purple glasses. I was impressed at how she facilitated the combative audition environment yet somehow managed to put us at ease. When I left that final audition to board the Short Line bus back to camp, I'd made up my mind to become a casting director one day and share a brownstone in the West Village with my best friends from theater camp. Though ABC chose the

* Stagedoor Manor is a performing arts summer camp located in Loch Sheldrake, New York. Over the past thirty-six years, it has trained thousands of young actors, many of whom have gone on to success in film, television, and theater.

other girl for my role, by some twist of fate, she turned the movie down after receiving a better offer for a Disney Sunday night movie. ABC asked me to audition one more time, so my devoted parents picked me up from theater camp at two in the morning and dropped me off at my manager's apartment. Then they drove to western Massachusetts to attend visiting day at my sister's music camp. My tireless parents were awake for about twenty-four hours, and it also happened to be their wedding anniversary that day. They wanted to help make my dreams come true, even if it meant sacrificing sleep.

When I got back to Stagedoor after the audition, there was a phone message waiting for me from my manager. I got the part!

1985: Here I am on set (far right) with the other child actors in the ABC Afterschool Special. Note my bow tie, feathered hair, and trademark purple glasses.

My college years, 1991. The ring in my nose and scarves were my signature look. This is right around the time I played Ophelia.

I spent the next ten years as a young working actor in New York City. Stints included *Sesame Street*, a bologna commercial that ran for years, and numerous plays for the Young Playwrights Festival at Playwrights Horizons. I had a fierce competitive streak that helped me overcome most audition rejection, except when I got close to getting cast on ABC's *Growing Pains* and in the role of the younger cousin in Neil Simon's hit Broadway play *Brighton Beach Memoirs*. Those were two lost parts that I never got over, and still haven't at age forty!

When I graduated high school, I decided to leave New York and my acting career to attend the University of Wisconsin. I thrived in Madison's vibe of political activism and the university's excellent history program. In my spare time, I performed in experimental theater productions in an old warehouse on the other side of town. I played Ophelia in an uncut version of *Hamlet* which was called *Hamlet the Miniseries, Parts 1 and 2*. A bearded anthropology major I'd really liked had just ditched me, so I worked through my anger playing Ophelia as a cocaine-snorting blues singer dressed in combat boots and a Joy Division T-shirt. When I wasn't playing Ophelia, I played Guildenstern using a puppet who talked in a falsetto voice. The actor who played Hamlet was often naked, and the entire "To be or not to be" speech consisted of him undressing, which viewers found either distracting or, in my mother's case, extremely enjoyable. I wrote scathing theater reviews for the school's daily *Badger Herald* newspaper, inspired by my idols Frank Rich and John Simon. When I mailed my clippings back to my parents, my mother politely suggested I ease up on my criticism and reminded me that I was reviewing university theater productions, not Broadway.

During school breaks, I interned for Meg Simon Casting and Marcia Shulman Casting. Today Meg is the vice president in charge of casting for Warner Bros. in New York, and Marcia spent many years as executive vice president in charge of casting for the Fox Broadcasting Company in L.A. Both women continue to serve as casting mentors to me.

After graduating from Wisconsin in 1994, I moved back to New York City, but neither Meg nor Marcia was hiring an assistant. I was equally interested in casting, directing, acting, producing, and writing. My father suggested I take a yellow legal pad and write down a list of career goals. My mother encouraged me to audition for a few more years so I wouldn't have regrets later on. I called an agent whom I'd freelanced with when I was younger, and she began to send me out on auditions.

To support myself, I temped at Citibank and Grey Advertising, made espresso at Barnes & Noble, and taught Hebrew school. In 1995, I dressed as the Cat in the Hat in the Macy's Thanksgiving Day Parade, waving to the packed crowds from my parade float, then spent Christmas season parading around Macy's in the cat suit. I had my own dressing room at Macy's (in reality a large supply closet), and this gave me an elevated status compared to the hundreds of actors employed as Santa's elves who had to share one common dressing room. I'd pass them by in my cat suit, certain they were hissing at me.

With my parents as the Cat in the Hat. Macy's, 1995. When I shook my furry cat tail at my father, I heard him mutter to my mother, "We spent thousands of dollars on theater camp and acting lessons for this?"

Epiphany #2: Crawling Around Pretending to Be a Dog

My second and final casting director epiphany occurred in the late 1990s. My agent called with an appointment for a regional production of the hit off-Broadway play *Sylvia*, by A. R. Gurney Jr. Sarah Jessica Parker had just played the title role of a talking dog named Sylvia. Stephanie Klapper was the casting director.* She'd seen me audition as a child and was confident

---

* For some major productions, the process of selecting actors for sometimes hundreds of parts requires specialized staff. A *casting director*, or "CD," is in charge of most of the daily work involved in this process during preproduction. A CD is sometimes assisted by a casting associate, and productions with large numbers of extras may have their own extras casting director. The CD acts as a liaison between director, actors and their agents/managers, and the studio/network to get the characters in the script cast.

enough to bring me straight into the session attended by the director. Big mistake.

I wasn't motivated and hadn't spent time preparing the scenes. I tried to hide this by crawling around the filthy audition-room floor attempting to "bark" and "sit." After a loud bark, I met Stephanie's eyes. She was clearly mortified. It was pretty obvious how little I cared about acting at that point. She nodded politely as I snuck out of the audition room. In a state of shock, I walked up Sixth Avenue and ceremoniously tossed my box of expensive head shots into a trash can. Epiphany #2: my acting career was officially over.

Susan Lucci Goes to Voice Mail: My Life as an Assistant

I spent the next several years slaving away as an assistant at a reputable bicoastal talent agency and later on at a busy commercial casting office. Since this was the late 1990s, JPGs and PDFs had yet to be invented. Casting tapes had to be dubbed in real time onto three-quarter-inch or VHS tapes, then delivered to various producers long after FedEx closed for the evening. Assistants had to photocopy and fax all audition scripts. The machines were often jammed, and the phones rang off the hook. There was no way to win.

I worked for a newly promoted powerhouse talent agent. My salary was $450 a week, with very long hours and no overtime pay. I could barely afford my rent in Brooklyn and subsisted on hard-boiled eggs and rice cakes. One of the commercial agents suggested I bring in a plate so that I'd feel more civilized when eating lunch at my desk. And when another commercial agent found me buried on a Sunday at the office, catching up on talent deal memos, he said: "You're going to go very far one day."

The agency's newest client was Susan Lucci from *All My Children*, and my boss was her primary agent. I was instructed to always put Ms. Lucci's call through, no matter what. One day I stepped away to use the bathroom, and Susan Lucci went to voice mail. I was reprimanded in the hallway and was certain I'd be fired. Jack Romano, our legendary acting teacher from Stagedoor Manor, had often said: "You have to be superhuman to be in show business." At that moment in the hallway, I realized I was hardly superhuman. Instead, I was flat broke and exhausted. It was then that I realized how much I wanted to be back on the creative side of the business: I wanted to work in casting.

Can You Hear Me Now?

I left the talent agency to work as a casting associate for a busy commercial casting office. My salary was now a whopping $500 a week (which doesn't go too far in New York City) with no health insurance. Right after September 11, 2001, we got hired to cast the "Can You Hear Me Now?" campaign for a new company called Verizon. We were looking for a spokesman who was different from the Sprint businessman and Carrot Top in the AT&T spots. I auditioned hundreds of actors, of all ages and diverse ethnic backgrounds, saying, "Can you hear me now?" for weeks on end. I'll share more on how we cast that famous part in chapter 8 when I talk about auditioning for commercials.

In 2002, I cast the entire season of plays for the prestigious Ensemble Studio Theatre. I set up a desk amid the dusty costumes and mismatched shoes in a storage closet and cast plays for esteemed playwrights like Horton Foote. The *New York Times* raved about the actors I'd cast, so I had some praiseworthy reviews to add to my résumé, but I was still flat broke and barely surviving on plain bagels and cheap white wine. New York City was trying to recover from September 11. It was a dark, bleak time for all of us, and I was desperate for a life change.

My Seven Years as a Disney Princess:
Making Animals Talk and Mermaids Sing

In 2002, I was hired for a few weeks to assist with the New York casting on Chris Rock's movie *Head of State*. At one point, the L.A. casting director turned to me at the table read* and said, "You're so ambitious. You should come to L.A. You'd be really successful out there." My father had enough airline miles to book me a free flight, and I began to set up some meetings in advance of the trip. Then I panicked. Though I'd gotten my driver's license in Wisconsin, I'd had no experience driving a car, and certainly not in L.A. My father insisted that this trip was not the time for me to learn to drive. "You can't show up frazzled to your meetings. It's not cute. Time is money, especially in Los Angeles." So, despite my protestations, my father offered to pay for a car service for my ten days of meetings. He said it was an investment in my career and that I could pay him back later.

I reconnected with Donna Morong, a former acting teacher from my teen years, who at that time was a casting executive at Walt Disney Pictures in Burbank, California. She mentioned that Walt Disney Animation Studios was searching for a new casting director, and they wanted to hire someone who knew theater actors. She faxed my résumé over, and I soon engaged in six long interviews with multiple producers in the animation division and racked up nearly a thousand dollars in car service fees. A few weeks later, Disney called with the official job offer. The company relocated me to sunny Los Angeles in September 2002, a year after the twin towers collapsed and a month shy of my thirtieth birthday.

During my five years in Los Angeles working at Walt Disney Animation Studios, I quickly learned the politics of being a studio casting executive. I began to navigate the L.A. freeways, enjoy sushi power lunches with top talent agents, and do studio coverage for comedy festivals and the Sundance Film Festival. I also watched the animation division transition from traditional, hand-drawn (2-D) animated movies into computer-animated (3-D) movies. We started hiring celebrities to voice the characters in order to stay competitive with rival animation studios. I cast some wonderful

---

* The *table read, table work, or read-through,* is when the actors with speaking parts gather around a table and read through the screenplay or script.

films while on staff at Disney, including *The Incredibles*, *Chicken Little*, *Brother Bear*, and *The Princess and the Frog*. And of course I paid my father back the money for the car service.

In 2007, I moved back to New York to oversee casting and talent development for Disney's theatrical division. My job entailed traveling around the country conducting open talent calls for children and adults for *The Lion King* and *Mary Poppins*. I organized a ten-city search to find a new young ingenue for the lead role of Ariel in *The Little Mermaid* on Broadway. I'll share more about this job in later chapters. Sadly, after the 2008 economic crisis, several of Disney's Broadway shows closed. After seven years at Disney, my position was dissolved in August 2009.

Recession Fairy Tales: The Birth of Jen Rudin Casting

Several months after leaving Disney, I officially opened Jen Rudin Casting. Today I cast for films, television shows, and animated movies in New York and Los Angeles. The best part of my job is casting someone in their first big role. Just before Thanksgiving in 2011, I was hired to do a casting search for a five-year-old version of the nine-year-old lead actress in a film for Universal Pictures called *Mama*, starring Jessica Chastain, executive produced by Guillermo del Toro. They'd done an extensive casting search in Canada and had not been successful. I auditioned more than seventy girls between the ages of two and seven and videotaped twenty little girls for the director and producers to view on location in Toronto. They chose a focused, smart five-year-old named Morgan McGarry. When I called Morgan with the amazing news, I said the magic words that every actor dreams of: "Guess what? You got the part!"

There's no direct path to success in show business. Unlike most professions, you don't get an advanced degree in acting that comes with the promise of a job. Auditions are competitive, time consuming, and can be expensive to attend. There are multiple elements that an actor can't control:

Me with Morgan McGarry at the 2012 New York premiere of Mama.

last-minute auditions, the traffic to get to the audition, the long wait in the waiting room, the director who texts during your scene. Your job as an actor is to control the elements you can and be as prepared as possible. To thrive in this exciting, constantly changing, and completely unpredictable world, you must stay focused and organized while constantly managing expectations. If you want to be a professional actor, this book will offer you tips to succeed in the audition room—the first step toward getting the part.

I love being a casting director. We're not the producer, writer, director, studio executive, or choreographer. We're consultants hired to organize, research, and identify the actors for the play, movie, or television show. We present actors to the director and producer and work together as a team to choose the most qualified actors to populate the world of the project. Some days my job is easy and everyone collaborates and agrees on who to hire. During the more challenging times of the casting process I often play the role of a therapist, confidante, diplomat, or mediator, trying to balance the needs of everyone involved.

Today I get to work with legendary directors such as Peter Bogdanovich. Here we are doing auditions in 2013 for his movie Squirrels to the Nuts. (BECKY CHICOINE)

As a former actor who now sits on the other side of the casting table, I wrote this book for all actors to help you navigate the audition process. Trust me, I've seen it all, and I'm here to share the good and the bad, practical tips, and advice to give you the best preparation possible to succeed. The rest is up to you.

CHAPTER ONE

THE INITIAL INVESTMENT

My parents spent a *lot* of money for me to pursue my professional acting career. I took voice lessons, acting workshops, and voice-over classes, and went to Stagedoor Manor for six summers. Every year my father would grumble as he wrote the check for theater camp, but my parents encouraged my creativity, no matter what the cost.

If you want to become a professional actor, you need to invest wisely in your career. An acting career costs money. Prepare to make endless sacrifices, both monetary and emotional. In pursuing these expensive dreams, there will be many unglamorous steps along the way. The audition process is filled with daily highs and lows, yet the possibility of landing a dream role is what propels actors to keep auditioning. It's hard not to get carried away in the fantasy, but you will likely go on hundreds, if not thousands, of auditions before you earn a penny. No one pays you to go on an audition. Look at your acting career as a marathon, not a sprint.

Opening a Cigar Store

Vocal coach Bob Marks shared this analogy with me: "If you want to open a cigar store, you need initial investment money. It takes money to rent the store location, buy a cash register, start to advertise, and buy cigars." Think of your acting career like that cigar store, as a start-up business. When first starting out, you'll need initial seed money.

To jump-start your career, begin by making a list of start-up costs. Here's what you'll need to invest in:

- Head shots taken by a professional photographer
- Professional head shot prints and postcards
- Acting lessons—both group and private coaching (it's important to have both)
- Workshops to meet agents and casting directors
- Acting intensives
- Vocal coaching
- Dance classes
- Subscriptions to reputable audition listings (examples include *Backstage* newspaper, www.backstage.com, Actors Access, and Casting Networks)
- Transportation (bus, train, subway, gas, parking, toll) costs to get to auditions
- Extra money for that Starbucks latte or snack during long audition days

If you're still in school, your parents will (hopefully) help you pursue your dreams, as mine did. If you're an adult, you're in charge of managing your own finances. I suggest that you have an amount in your head that you are willing to spend. How much can you truly afford? Be honest about your potential. If you're not careful, you can really break the bank. Decide up front how much money you want to invest right away. This will help assuage the pain when the costs start to add up. You don't need to spend a lot of money for success, but you do need to spend money on good training to gain more confidence when you walk into audition. The ends justify the means.

At this early stage, you need to make sure that you really want to be an actor and that you're not just an impulse buyer.

Who Am I, Anyway?

Now that you've created your budget, it's time to get your head shot* and résumé assembled. If you're calling yourself a professional actor, you need a professional head shot so you can start to submit for work. Your head shot is your business card. The photo must look like YOU. Take a quick look in the mirror. What do you see? What color is your hair? Is it curly or straight? Do you wear contacts or glasses, or both depending on the day? Your head shot needs to reflect you as you really are (with a little professional re-touching to enhance what you already have!).

An excellent head shot will cost you money. What makes a great photo? Everything from your outfit and makeup to the setting, lighting, and of course, your smile. Your photo should represent you on your best day. It's always disappointing when an actor comes to an audition and looks nothing like his or her head shot.

AUDITION STORIES

My First Audition

My first audition was for a Stella D'oro cookies commercial. I looked right into the camera and yelled "Stella!" I booked that one and got my SAG card.

—BONNIE ROSE,
www.BonnieRoseNY.com

---

* A *head shot* is a specific type of modern portrait for today's branding needs, where the focus of the photograph captures the personality of its subject.

How to Find a Head Shot Photographer

- Ask for recommendations from fellow actors.

- Check out photographers' websites.

- Narrow down your choices. Then make an appointment to visit each photographer's studio to meet them and see if you feel comfortable with their vibe. Note: there should be no charge for this meeting.

- At the meeting, look through their photography books.

- Ask the photographer for wardrobe requirements and ideas for what to wear at the shoot.

- See if the photographer can provide a stylist for hair and makeup. Usually photographers have someone they like to work with. It's worth the extra cost to have a professional there who can help you look your best.

- If you're on a tight budget, ask the photographer if they ever offer specials or seasonal discounts. Like them on Facebook or join their e-mail list so you can be the first to hear about any discounts.

- If you can't afford to pay the full price for head shots, try bartering a bit. Explain that you don't want to insult them but would love to find a way to make it work. It might not work, but it never hurts to ask.

— ASK THE — PHOTOGRAPHER

What makes a great head shot?

A great head shot reveals who you are. Confidence and accessibility are the yin and yang of a good head shot, and they must be in balance. Get plenty of sleep before your shoot. Have fun. Let go and you will naturally reveal your unique spirit.

—SHANDON YOUNGCLAUS,
owner, *Amazing Headshots*
(www.amazingheadshots.com),
Los Angeles

Sample Head Shots of Real Actors

To give you a sense of what professional head shots should look like, here are two excellent examples from actors that I've worked with:

(JORDAN MATTER)

I love Stephanie's photo because she looks beautiful and natural. She could play an assortment of roles—ingenue, best friend, young mom.

I would easily cast Peter as a lawyer, doctor, or businessman based on this photo. Peter told me his reasons for choosing this photo: "I thought it conveyed some strength and honesty with a hint of 'I'm still a regular kind of guy.' I thought it would be multifunctional, working well in theater, television, and film.

(TESS STEINKOLK)

It's an investment that's paid off well, as I get called in for television and theater on a regular basis."

— ASK THE — PHOTOGRAPHER

What makes a great head shot?

The most important thing is that the head shot look like the actor on a really good day. Everything today is so reality based that you don't want a head shot with all kinds of dramatic mood lighting. You want a head shot that looks like a real person, whether it's a serious (legit) or a smiling (commercial) head shot. Is the person expressing an emotion that they're really feeling? Are they communicating a real thought?

—DOUGLAS GORENSTEIN,
Douglas Gorenstein Photography
(www.douglasgorenstein.com),
New York

Choosing Your Head Shots

After your photo shoot, your photographer will send you a digital link or DVD to view your photos. Now comes the overwhelming task of narrowing down your head shot choices. Ideally, you want to have two or three photos:

- A happy commercial shot (bright colors, great smile)

- A more serious shot for theater and film

- A wild card—a photo that you love and will use once in a while when a great role comes up

— HEAD SHOT DOS AND DON'TS —

👍 DO work with your photographer to narrow down your choices.

👍 DO get some professional opinions about your photos. If you don't have an agent or manager guiding you, ask a few trusted friends and family members.

👍 DO be selective when sharing your top choices and gathering opinions.

👍 DO keep perspective. Your mother's views may add to your stress. Take all opinions with a grain of salt.

👍 DO e-mail the digital file of the photo to a reputable place for re-productions. You'll need some hard copies for auditions. Visit www.modernage.com or www.reproductions.com. Even if you don't live in the city where these companies are based, you can still e-mail them your digital files and have them process your photos, send you test prints, and ship the completed prints to you.

👎 DON'T post the link to your proofs on Facebook. Having your thousands of friends comment will *not* help you select your photo.

👎 DON'T try to save money by taking your own photos or, worse, paying someone with a digital camera who is unqualified and inexperienced.

👎 DON'T be cheap and print copies at Walgreens. You're a profes-sional actor. Be classy. Spend money where it matters.

Formatting Your Résumé

You need to take a résumé as well as a head shot to each audition. Your résumé should include the following four sections (in this sequence):

1. Header (includes name, contact info, physical description, and union affiliations)

2. Experience

3. Training

4. Skills

Clearly label each of these sections (except the header) on your résumé. Check out the sample résumés on the following pages for format and content. Use them as guides as you work on your own. Note the clear, organized listing of all their credits.

—— RÉSUMÉ DOS AND DON'TS ——

👍 DO include a mobile contact number. Record a clear and professional outgoing voice mail message. Treat your cell phone as your work phone number. This is not the place to be cute or funny.

👍 DO include an e-mail address and/or website information. Use a Gmail address that's clear and simple. CuteGirlz431@aol.com is NOT a professional e-mail address. If you have a complicated last name like Camadeco, keep it simple, like LaurenCo212@gmail.com.

👍 DO staple your résumé to the back of your photo. This is a universal rule in casting. I can't tell you how many times an actor has offered me a photo and a résumé *not* stapled. If you can't follow this simple direction, how are you going to manage intricate rules on a movie set?

👎 DON'T include your home address, home phone number, or social security information on your résumé. Maybe it's because I watch too much *Law and Order*, but your home address shouldn't

214 W. 29th St.
Suite 1203
New York, NY 10001
212.977.8502
212.977.8420 (fax)
License Number: 0927158

Harden Curtis Associates

Stephanie Rothenberg

BROADWAY

HOW TO SUCCEED IN BUSINESS…	Rosemary	Rob Ashford Al Hirschfeld Theatre

WORLD PREMIERES

SENSE & SENSIBILITY, THE MUSICAL	Elinor Dashwood	Marcia Milgrom-Dodge Denver Center Theatre Company
ROMAN HOLIDAY	Princess Anne	John Miller-Stephany Guthrie Theater
FROG KISS	Princess Clementine	Kenneth Roberson Virginia Stage Company

NY READINGS

CASTLE WALK	Young Irene Castle	Richard Stafford
SOAPDISH: THE MUSICAL	Ensemble	Rob Ashford
THE UNSINKABLE MOLLY BROWN	Maud/Kit/Ensemble	Kathleen Marshall

VOICEOVER/RECORDING

Savva (Major Motion Picture)	Hot Girl 1 & 2	Glukoza Production Limited
The 99 Restaurant	Server	60: Radio Spot
The Tweenies	Fizz	BBC/Act IV Prod
Thoroughly Modern Millie Jr.	Millie	MTI
Disney's Beauty and The Beast Jr.	Belle	MTI/Disney JR.
Disney's High School Musical I and II	Kelsi	MTI
"Give This Christmas Away"	Background Vocalist	Matthew West feat. Amy Grant

EDUCATION
CAP21 (NYU/Tisch School of the Arts)

SPECIAL SKILLS
Dancer (jazz, modern, tap, ballet, pointe), Spanish (conversational)

214 West 29th Street
Suite 1203
New York, NY 10001
212.977.8502
212.977.8420 (fax)
License Number: 0927158

Harden-Curtis Associates

PETER RINI

TELEVISION

BLUE BLOODS	CBS Studios/CBS	Dir. JimMcKay
SMASH	Dreamworks/ NBC	Dir. Adam Bernstein, Tricia Brock
ER	John Wells Prods./NBC	Dir. Stephen Cragg
RESCUE ME	Apostle Prods./FX	Dir. John Fortenberry
LAW AND ORDER	Dick Wolf Prods./NBC	Dir. Gloria Muzio
LAW AND ORDER: CI	Dick Wolf Prods./NBC	Dir. Don Scardino
LAW AND ORDER: SVU	Dick Wolf Prods./NBC	Dir. Michael Knight
THE JURY	20th Century Fox TV/FOX	Dir. Jean de Segonzac
HACK	CBS Prods./CBS	Dir. Bob Singer
WHEN I GROW UP	ABC Productions	Dir. Tim Squyres
NOW AND AGAIN	CBS Productions	Dir. Vincent Misiano
SPIN CITY	Dreamworks SKG/ABC	Dir. Andy Cadiff
THIRD WATCH	John Wells Prods./NBC	Dir. Guy N. Bee
SEX AND THE CITY	Darren Star Prods./HBO	Dir. Nicole Holofcener

FILM

BOILER ROOM	New Line Cinema	Dir. Ben Younger
SLEEPERS	Warner Brothers	Dir. Barry Levinson
THE JUROR	Columbia Pictures	Dir. Brian Gibson

BROADWAY and NATIONAL TOUR

SOUTH PACIFIC (1ST national tour)	Harbison	Dir. Bart Sher
NEIL SIMON'S PROPOSALS	Vinnie (original company)	Dir. Joe Mantello
A VIEW FROM THE BRIDGE	Marco	Dir. Michael Mayer
TARTUFFE: BORN AGAIN	Agent Loyal	Dir. David Saint

OFF BROADWAY

THE OLD BOY	Sam	Keen Company/ Dir. Jonathan Silverstein
THE TALLS (World Premiere)	John Clarke	2ST Uptown/Dir. Carolyn Cantor
THINGS YOU SHOULDN'T SAY PAST MIDNIGHT	Gene	Promenade /Dir. John Rando
NAKED (w/Mira Sorvino)	Franco	CSC/Dir. John Rando
DEAD CITY	Husband	New Georges Theatre/Dir. Daniella Topol
THE MERCHANT OF VENICE	Balthazar	NYSF/Dir. Barry Edelstein
SOMEWHERE IN THE PACIFIC	Delucca	Playwrights Horizons/Dir. Mark Brokaw
PETER AND JERRY	Peter (cover)	2ST /Dir. Pam MacKinnon

REGIONAL

EDITH (world premiere)	Joseph Tumulty	Berkshire Theater Festival, Dir. Michael Sexton
GLENGARRY GLEN ROSS	Richard Roma	Dallas Theatre Center/Dir. David Kennedy
AN ENEMY OF THE PEOPLE	Horstrer	Shakespeare Theatre, DC/Dir. Kjetil Bang-Hansen
TWO GENTLEMEN OF VERONA	Thurio	Shakespeare Theatre, DC/Dir. Doug Wager
MUCH ADO ABOUT NOTHING	Don Pedro	Shakespeare Theatre, DC/Dir. Mark Lamos
THE PROVOK'D WIFE	Constant	A. R. T./Dir. Mark Wing-Davey
HEAVEN CAN WAIT	Joe Pendleton	Westport Country Playhouse/ Dir. Joe Grifasi
ROBBERS (w/Judd Hirsch)	Ted	Long Wharf/ Dir. Marshall Mason

TRAINING

M.F.A. New York University Graduate Acting Program
B.A. Theatre Arts, Brandeis University

Katie Balen

RKS MANAGEMENT | 212-717-2716

Height: 63"   Weight: 110 lbs   Eyes: Blue   Hair: Blonde Hair Length: Long

Broadway National Tour
Mary Poppins   Jane Banks   Disney

Commercials/Voiceovers
(List Available Upon Request)

Film
Not Fade Away   Grace's Sister   Paramount Pictures

Regional Theatre
Willy Wonka	Veruca Salt	Yorktown Stage
Bye Bye Birdie	Rosie	KJK Productions
Grease	Sandy	Random Farms Kids Theater
The Secret Garden	Mary Lennox	Random Farms Kids Theater
Willy Wonka	Veruca Salt	Hornet Hive Productions
Annie	Tessie	Hornet Hive Productions

Television
Tonight Show with Conan O'Brien   Performance   NBC

Appearances
The Grove, Los Angeles	Performance	KOST 103.5
KOST Radio, Los Angeles	Performance	KOST 103.5
It's My Life	Interview	PBS Kids
Talk Back, Los Angeles	Interview	Press Briefing
Kids Night on Broadway, LA	Self/Autographs	Kids Night on
Broadway National		
Program		
Arizona Teen Magazine	Interview	AZ Teen Magazine

Training
Voice	Badiene Magaziner, Monica Robinson, Robert Marks, Amelia DeMayo
Acting	New York Film Academy, The Barrows Group, Denise Simon,
Dance	Westchester Performing Arts, Rose Menendez

Special Skills

Singer, Dancer, Actor, Improve Character creation: Ballet, Hip Hop, Tap. Vocal Range: Soprano, Vocal Style: Pop, Belt, Legit, Voiceover: Accent: British, New York. Special skills include: Self taught Piano and Guitar, softball, volleyball, cheerleading, Girl Scouts, Academics: Honor Roll Student 2013, IBM Science Program, Wonderful with young children.

be floating around for anyone to potentially see. If you book the role, the production can reach you or your agent via cell or e-mail to obtain your home address and phone number.

- DON'T lie about ANYTHING—your height or weight, training, roles you have played, or directors you've worked with. Everyone knows everyone in this industry, and you WILL get caught.

Remember, every audition is a job interview. Your résumé must be professional, organized, and perfectly formatted. There's no excuse for sloppiness!

STAGE MOMS' CORNER

Photos and Résumés

Photographers often charge less for children. And since children change and grow quickly, you may have to budget for new head shots every few years or so. Make sure the photo looks like your child—young, happy, and smiling. DON'T go crazy with hair and makeup. Save that for *Toddlers & Tiaras*. When crafting a résumé for your child, keep the following points in mind:

- Keep the résumé simple. Less is more, especially when your child is just starting out. Local roles in school, church, and community theater productions are perfectly legitimate credits.

- Be careful not to put anything indicating where you live. Instead of listing your child's school, just list the auditorium's name. This is just a safety precaution in case the résumé ends up in the wrong hands.

- List acting, voice, and dance teachers. Casting directors can easily pick up the phone to call a reputable acting teacher on the résumé and ask if your child is focused and disciplined (or not).

- Don't lie about height, weight, or special skills.

AUDITION STORIES

My First Audition

My first audition was for a commercial. They were looking for a "Sexy Woman." I put on a brand-new, very tight skirt and marched out the door. Needless to say, an integral part of the audition was to strut my stuff "runway-model style," and unfortunately, all I could do was wobble like a penguin in that overly tight skirt. And no, I did not get the part.

—ANNA LAKOMY,
www.annalakomy.org

How to Find Out About Auditions

When we are ready to begin casting, casting directors will release a casting breakdown that lists all open roles for the project. Here's a sample casting breakdown so you can familiarize yourself with the format:

Wednesday, Feb. 15, 2012, 7:45 AM Pacific

HOW TO LIVE WITH YOUR PARENTS FOR THE REST OF YOUR LIFE (Working Title)	Exec. Producers: Claudia Lonow, Brian Grazer, Francie Calfo
Pilot	Writer: Claudia Lonow
½ Hour	NY Casting Director: Jen Rudin
AFTRA	LA Casting Director: Susan Edelman
Imagine Television and 20th Century Fox TV for ABC	LA Casting Associate: Christina Snider
	Start Date: o/a mid March
	Location: Los Angeles

SUBMIT ELECTRONICALLY

To download the script, go to www.screenplayonline.com and use script key code: 203claudia21

POLLY - CAST: SARAH CHALKE

[ELAINE] Polly's mom, mid-50s to mid 60s, very attractive, always optimistic and outspoken, Elaine can never say no to herself. Elaine came of age during the late '70s - '80s and has never really left that self-absorbed, irreverent era behind her. As Polly puts it, "Most people have a voice in their head that says, 'look before you leap.' My mother's voice says, 'look at me, I'm leaping!'" Elaine is unapologetic about her unabashed need for attention--in fact, Elaine is unapologetic about pretty much everything...SERIES REGULAR (1)

[MAX] Mid-50s to mid-60s, Polly's stepfather, married to Elaine, always in motion, explosive, Max owns a nightclub and is, as Polly puts it, the world's most resentful cancer survivor (he blames Elaine for not stopping the surgeons from taking his testicle; she thinks having just one looks distinguished). Max loves Elaine (and Polly and Natalie) but is more down-to-earth, practical and clear-sighted than she is; he's also less selfish, and doesn't mind giving up theatre tickets so they can babysit for Natalie while Polly goes out...SERIES REGULAR (1)

[JULIAN] Mid to late 30s, Polly's "Big Lebowski-esque" ex-husband, the kind of guy who doesn't pay his bills unless they're in a red envelope, Julian likes his gadgets, like the "life hammer" that can be used if your car goes underwater, and he's always coming by to tell Polly about a new smartphone app. Julian is a fixture in Polly and Natalie's lives because, as he tells Max, "I need to be there for her and Natalie 'cause I wasn't before"...SERIES REGULAR (6)

[NATALIE] 6, a "Little Miss Sunshine", she has a special connection with each character and appears to be getting the best each adult has to offer. Natalie thinks she's afraid of dogs, but all that changes when her grandparents get her a puppy. **PLEASE INDICATE DATE OF BIRTH ON SUBMISSION**...SERIES REGULAR (1)

[GREGG] 30s, good-natured, smart, appealing, Polly's best friend and boss at Pantry Pete's, Gregg's married but is the kinda guy Polly's been looking for all her life but was too screwed up to attract. Gregg's supportive of Polly's upcoming date and goes with her and her assistant Jenn to help her pick out a dress...**PLEASE SUBMIT ALL ETHNICITIES.** SERIES REGULAR (7)

[JENN] 20s, Polly's assistant, she's cool, fun and single. Polly views herself as Jenn's mentor, but Jenn sees Polly as a cautionary tale. They become friends and partners in crime. Jenn sets up Polly with her recently divorced, "fragile" brother, Luke. **PLEASE SUBMIT ALL ETHNICITIES**...SERIES REGULAR (9)

[LUKE] 30s, Jenn's brother, very cute, recently divorced and emotionally fragile, Luke goes out on a date with Polly but is a little anxious beforehand so he takes an ativan--which doesn't go well with the series of drinks he has on the date itself. Luke gets really wasted and has to be driven home by Max and Julian. PLEASE SUBMIT ALL ETHNICITIES...GUEST STAR (18)

[CHILD POLLY] Polly seen as a child in the 1970s, she's exposed to a few things that she shouldn't be thanks to her hippie parents. She's also seen at home with a snarling dog chained to the radiator...no lines, 3 scenes (4)

[CLUB GOER #1] This male club goer in a bad part of town takes offense when Luke makes a comment to him...1 line, 1 scene (23)

STORY LINE: Newly single mom POLLY returns home to her mom ELAINE and stepdad MAX, with her 5 year old daughter NATALIE in tow, to try to put the pieces of her life back together, maybe have a d-a-t-e, and be to Natalie the mother she never had for herself, or as she likes to put it, the best single working mom in the universe...

Agents and managers subscribe to Breakdown Services, which, in the old days, delivered physical copies of the breakdowns to the offices of agents and managers each morning. The agents and managers would go through all the projects actively casting and type a cover letter to the casting director suggesting various clients for each role. They'd messenger over a package with the submission letter and photos and résumés to the casting office. Today, breakdowns and submissions are all done digitally. Agents can easily click through and submit clients for parts all day as the breakdowns come out.

There are also many online audition and casting resources available directly to actors, such as Actors Access,* Backstage.com, or Casting Networks.† Google these sites, sign up for an account, then create your actor profile. The fees are manageable. Once your profile's complete, you'll begin to receive casting notices. You can click and submit yourself for posted projects. Many films and theater projects will be for nonpaying or tiny-stipend nonunion jobs. But they can provide valuable experience, especially when you're just starting out.

Traveling for Auditions

If you don't live in New York City or Los Angeles, you'll have to travel for auditions. Remember to add in the cost of flights, hotel rooms, food, taxicabs, subways, gas, parking, and bridge and tunnel tolls to your initial budget estimate. We'll go over more specifics of New York versus L.A. in chapter 11.

---

* Actors Access is a website connected to Breakdown Services that allows actors to self-submit for auditions without an agent. Visit www.actorsaccess.com.

† Casting Networks is another site to sign up and submit for auditions. Visit www.castingnetworks.com for more details. Sometimes a project will be listed on multiple sites, but not always.

Consider a Flexible Job

A corporate job deserves your attention, just like an acting career. You can't have it both ways. Find a job that's flexible so you can be available to audition. Make sure to tell your employers that you're an actor so there's no surprise when you need to run out of the workplace for a last-minute commercial audition.

I once had to leave a temp assignment at Citibank to rush downtown for a callback for a national Cascade commercial. As I ran out of the office applying my lipstick, the senior vice president of global asset management screamed, "Fire her! Fire the temp agency!"

Flexible Jobs 101

- Waitress, bartender, hostess at a restaurant, barista
- Childcare: nanny or babysitter
- Teaching: tutor, acting instructor in schools
- Fitness: front-desk attendant at a gym or yoga studio (bonus: you might even get a free membership!)
- Tour guide, personal assistant, theater usher, box office salesperson

So now you know what you need to get started. Here's a more detailed look at a sample budget:

- *Professional head shots with a professional photographer:* $700 and up. For kids, somewhere around $400.

- *Professional head shot prints and postcards:* fifty prints for $99.50 (head shots) and $89.00 for postcards. Prices may change but that's the rate at the time of this publication.

- *Acting lessons—group or private coaching:* private coaching runs about $100 to $200 per hour; group classes may charge monthly or semester fees depending on location and instructors.

- *Workshops to meet agents and casting directors:* prices start around $25 per workshop and go up depending on class size and length of workshop.

- *Audition Bootcamp/Master Class Intensives:* weekend workshop prices vary (anywhere from $200 to $1,000) depending on city and instructors.

- *Vocal coaching:* between $50 and $200 per hour.

- *Dance classes:* single classes are typically around $16, and a ten-class card is about $160 on average at places like Broadway Dance Center* and STEPS.† These are both New York–based studios; dance class costs can vary greatly from city to city.

- *Subscriptions to audition listings* (Backstage *newspaper, Actors Access, Casting Networks):* $50 per year. Playbill.com has a casting and jobs link that's free.

- *Transportation (bus, train, subway, gas, parking, toll) costs to travel to and from auditions:* prices will vary by city, but in New York expect parking and tolls to cost $50 a day and in L.A., around $10 for valet parking or $5 to $10 for public parking after the first two hours (which are usually free with parking validation). A single

---

* Broadway Dance Center: www.broadwaydancecenter.com
† Steps: www.stepsnyc.com

ride on a New York City bus or subway is $2.75 at the time of this publication (though there are discounts when you buy a multiride pass). A bus or Metro Rail ride in L.A. costs $1.50, but most people drive.

Extra money for that Starbucks latte before the audition: $4 to $5.

TOTAL START-UP COSTS: $1,000 and up

JEN'S LAST WORD

" It's better to pad your budget and overestimate your costs so you won't find yourself running out of money. Update your budget frequently and move money allocations from one budget line to another depending on your needs and where you notice yourself spending more or less. Costs will change depending on what your current needs are. Once you see the numbers all lined up and start sticking to a set budget, you'll feel more in control of your spending and ready to get out there and audition!

CHAPTER TWO

AGENTS AND MANAGERS 101

In 1982 I was discovered by Jean Fox and Adrienne Albert when they saw me in a Stagedoor Manor production of *Free to Be . . . You and Me*. Jean and Adrienne had recently partnered to form a management company called Kids & Company, which later became Fox Albert Management. Over the years, Jean and Adrienne launched the careers of Mira Sorvino, Josh Charles, Lacey Chabert, Timothy Olyphant, and many more. They represented me for eight years, until I went to college.

You don't necessarily need an agent or a manager when you're first starting to audition. But in the long run, obtaining representation should be a goal for all actors who want to seriously pursue this career.

Meeting Agents, Managers, and Casting Directors

Show business is like any other profession: networking is key. Sometimes you need to pay to network. For a reasonable fee, you can meet agents, managers, and casting directors at places like One on One,* Actors Connection,† and TVI Actors Studio.‡ These career networking companies are great resources for actors, especially if you're brand new to New York

---

* www.oneononenyc.com

† www.actorsconnection.com

‡ www.tvistudios.com

or Los Angeles. Visit their websites. For young actors, check out The Broadway Workshop* for musical theater classes and ACTeen† for TV and film training. They often have agents, managers, and casting directors attend showcases or final performances.

The Million-Dollar Question: How to Get an Agent

This is the most commonly asked question, and the answer is different for every actor. In the pre-Internet days, Ross Reports published a list of contacts that was updated frequently and contained mailing labels for agents and casting directors. Today you can start by researching talent agencies in major cities, such as New York, Los Angeles, Chicago, Toronto, Miami, Nashville, Dallas, or Denver. Each agency will note its submission requirements on its website, and some sites list the names of specific agents who work there. Make sure to read through all the requirements. Some agencies accept e-mail submissions while others may ask for a cover letter and hard copy of your photo and résumé. Every agency will be different. Remember to always proofread your cover letters. There's nothing more unprofessional and insulting then typing the wrong name or agency in the letter because you were too lazy to double-check when you cut and pasted. I've gotten so many letters over the years that either had my name misspelled or were addressed to the wrong company. One day at Disney, I got so fed up that I asked my intern to contact each actor who wrote an incorrect letter to point out their mistake. I figured we were doing them a favor in the long run.

Miley's Big Break

Mitchell Gossett, senior vice president at CESD Talent Agency in New York and Los Angeles, met Miley Cyrus when she was ten

---

* www.broadwayworkshop.com
† http://www.acteen.com

years old. At the time, Mitchell was working with another actor in Nashville, Tennessee, which boasts a huge Christian music scene. He had earned respect within the tight-knit Nashville community, and he got a call about meeting with Billy Ray Cyrus's daughter. Mitchell was invited to dinner at a Cyrus family friend's house, where Billy Ray wanted to feel him out. Once Mitchell and Billy Ray connected, Billy Ray called for ten-year-old Miley to come into the room and sing. Mitchell thought, *That's a very unusual voice.* He recalls that she sounded like a cabaret singer, as if she'd been singing in the clubs for a decade. Mitchell started to work with Miley, and he recalls, "Miley taped her *Hannah Montana* audition with her acting coach in Nashville three times. When I watched her final audition tape, my mouth dropped open. In that audition I saw a transformation that I couldn't explain. She was able to surprise even herself in the audition. Miley didn't just come in and create. She came in and reinvented. I knew this would be a game changer. When you surprise yourself as an actor, your audience is also surprised." Miley got cast in the lead role of Disney's *Hannah Montana,* and the rest, as they say, is history.

What Does an Agent Do?

Think of your talent agent as an employment agency. His or her job is to get you acting work. An agent also defends, supports, and promotes your interests. To do this, a talent agent must be familiar with you, to know what kind of work you can and cannot do in order to match you with various jobs.

Agencies commission 10 percent of whatever money the actor earns. Sometimes an agency will start out by freelancing with you. Then, if you book a job, they may offer you a standard one-year contract with an option to renew. A contract protects the agent by ensuring that you aren't going to go off to try to find another agent. Plus, the contract agreement means that the agency is entitled to collect the 10 percent of your earnings on any job you booked while represented by them.

A year is a very short amount of time to have a contract with an agency. Some agents don't expect an actor to book a job in the first year. They're looking at you as developmental at this point in time. Agents never get paid any money up front, so if any agent asks for upfront money, do not work with them or the agency. Whether an agent asks you to sign a contract or wants to freelance, you should feel encouraged. You're building relationships, and a freelance relationship is often the first step in acquiring representation.

STAGE MOMS' CORNER

Finding an Agent for Your Child

If you're looking for a talent agent for your child, often a professional head shot isn't necessary and a school photograph will do. If you have a résumé to accompany the photo and cover letter, send it, though it's not necessary at this beginning stage. If you're mailing in a cover letter with your child's photograph, be sure to include your child's name, date of birth, hair and eye color, height, weight, and any special skills. Be honest about their skills. Often talent agents who represent young actors don't require you to sign a contract. Instead they operate on a "verbal exclusive." They expect you to honor the verbal agreement and not seek representation elsewhere while they are working for you.

When an Agent Says "Let's Keep in Touch . . ."

An agent or manager might not be able to sign an actor for any of several reasons; for instance, if the agent already has other clients in the same age category, or if the agency is simply not signing anyone new. But if they ask the actor to keep in touch, they mean it. Often an agent will want to follow or keep track of an actor over a few years. If the actor starts to generate some buzz from a play or a Sundance film that's garnered some attention, the agent may then be interested in signing.

— ASK THE —
ACTOR
★

How did you get your agent, and how long have you worked together?

I met my agents at a presentation evening set up by my graduate school program at the University of California, San Diego. I was hoping to get a few interviews with agents after the presentation, but I got very lucky that evening and managed to get interest from more than twenty! So I was in the unusual position of interviewing agents as opposed to them interviewing me. After many meetings, the agents I chose were the Gage Group in New York. They were relaxed, interested in my life as well as my career, and they really got me. That was 1990. I am still with the same agency and I am still as sure of my decision as I was when I first met them.

—DANNY BURSTEIN,
four-time Tony-nominated actor

KEEPING IN TOUCH WITH AGENTS, MANAGERS, AND CASTING DIRECTORS: DOS AND DON'TS

👍 DO write when you have something to say. Share some good news: You've just completed Yale University's MFA program. You booked a Charmin commercial. You're costarring in an upcoming episode of *Law and Order: Special Victims Unit*. Be specific when you write.

👎 DON'T be overly creative in your letters. Less is more.

👎 DON'T stalk an agent or casting director's e-mail inbox by sending repetitive e-mails.

👎 DON'T send Facebook messages to a casting director.

👎 DON'T call an agent or casting director. You know the old saying "Don't call us, we'll call you"? It's true. Our days are very busy. Use mail and e-mail for correspondence. We'll call you when there's an audition for you. Be patient!

AGENT'S CORNER

What can a new client expect their first year in the business?

The first year is spent gaining fans, getting into the audition room, and building relationships with casting directors, directors, and writers. Take classes. Do a showcase where you can show those casting directors your work. This way, you don't walk into the audition room with the weight of the world on your shoulders every time, desperate to be hired. Instead, look at each audition as an opportunity to meet someone new to add to your fan base.

—MICHAEL KIRSTEN,
Harden-Curtis Associates

What Does a Manager Do?

A manager is an individual (or company) who guides and brings added value to the professional career of artists in the entertainment industry. The manager is responsible for overseeing the day-to-day business affairs of artists and advising and counseling them concerning professional matters, long-term plans, and personal decisions that may affect their career.

A manager helps with scheduling issues, which becomes important when you've got multiple auditions in one day. He or she reads scripts. When you're just starting out, a manager can get you in the door. Managers have time to call casting directors to get feedback on your auditions, and they can informally establish connections with producers and studios. Technically managers are not allowed to procure work for actors or negotiate contracts—that's the agent's job—but they often do, and they can also help their clients find an agent or decide when to leave their current agent and how to find a new one. A manager gets paid 10 to 15 percent of the client's earnings. Often they will want to commission the actor's earnings on all jobs, including commercials and voice-overs. The larger percentage is because they are supposed to be focusing on the "added value" concept. Keep in mind that having both an agent and a manager can cost you as much as 25 percent in commissions.

Because of the big picture and added value concepts, a manager may offer an actor a three-year contract instead of the typical one-year contract with an agent. Make sure you really like the manager before you sign. Have multiple meetings. How you want to proceed is completely your decision.

Getting locked into a three-year deal with a mediocre manager may be worse in the long run than having no manager at all.

The Agent or Manager Interview

Here are some questions to consider asking your potential agent or manager:

- How many clients do you represent?
- How many are my type (i.e., age, hair color, ethnicity)?
- Do you start by freelancing with an actor?
- How do you feel about a client continuing to submit for projects through Actors Access, Backstage.com, or Casting Networks? Will you want to commission a job I got on my own?
- Do you like my current headshots? If not, can you recommend any photographers?
- Who are your favorite acting, voice, or dance teachers? (An agent should never force you to go to a particular photographer or teacher, but they may have some whose work they admire or whom they have sent clients to over the years.)

An agent will often ask an actor the following questions:

- Which casting directors know you and your work? (Consider making a list in advance of the manager meeting, so you can share names.)
- What types of roles do you see yourself auditioning for?

You should be able to answer these questions confidently and clearly, so be sure to prepare your answers ahead of time.

Monologues

An agent may ask you to perform a monologue when you meet with him or her.

- Choose a monologue from a published play or screenplay. Do NOT perform a monologue you've written. Instead, go for writers like Neil Simon, Beth Henley, Nicky Silver, August Wilson, or John Patrick Shanley. No professional agent, casting director, or manager can assess your talent if they don't know the material. Visit www.samuelfrench.com. This site lists published plays and is a great resource for looking up titles.

- Know the author and the title of the play. You come off as flaky if you don't know this basic information.

- When performing your monologue, be clear who you're talking to. Sit or stand. Don't overblock your piece. For dramatic monologues, be careful of curse words and sexual content, as these could easily offend someone.

- No tears. Unless you are asked to perform a serious monologue, opt for one that's light and funny. Just because you can cry on cue doesn't mean you're the next Meryl Streep.

STAGE MOMS' CORNER

Often an interested agent or manager will interview your child first to get a sense of his or her personality. They want to see how your child interacts in a room with strangers, since this is essentially what happens when they go to an audition. After meeting with your child, they usually chat for a few minutes with the parent. This is your time to show the agent that you're a responsible and organized parent, and ready to make the commitment to start your child's career.

My agent pal Kerri Krilla at Cunningham-Escott-Slevin-Dipene Talent Agency (CESD) keeps a list of some of the funny lines she's heard when interviewing young actors. Her favorites include:

- "Do you think you'll invite me to your birthday party?"

- "Do you like this job? Do you get paid or is it just for fun?"

- "After I leave here I think I'll take a nap, because you asked a lot of questions!"

Of course, a child can get away with saying these adorable things. But these are not acceptable conversation points for an adult actor!

What do you look for when signing a new client?

Someone who has a lot of skills and can negotiate between genres. Someone who is personable and confident.

—DON BIRGE,
Stewart Talent,
www.stewarttalent.com, New York

JEN'S LAST WORD

" Meeting agents and managers can be a scary process for actors. You've got to learn how to master these meetings to keep moving forward in your career. Here's my advice:

- Be yourself.

- Do your research ahead of time so you know how many clients the agency represents and some of their well-known clients.

- Know your career goals and what you feel you can add to the equation. It's always easier for representation to service a client when each client, actor, and agent or manager has clear goals in mind.

- Flattery can go a long way. Pay an agent or manager a compliment if it's genuine: "I love your glasses" or "We share a mutual friend who says you're the best agent . . ."

- Smile, keep calm, and be confident!

CHAPTER THREE

LEAVE EARLY AND BRING A RAINCOAT

BASIC AUDITION PREP

I'm twelve years old and at the final audition for an off-Broadway play about a runaway girl. So much is riding on this particular callback. Starring in an off-Broadway play could potentially garner me a *New York Times* review. Plus, I want to prove to my manager that I can play more than just the funny friend. Then I see my nemesis across the waiting room: the stuck-up skinny girl from theater camp who often curls her hair at auditions with her portable curling iron. The girl who's already been a series regular on a short-lived TV show and just landed the coveted role of the abused daughter in a TV movie.

Our eyes lock. She waves at me, gliding over in her Benetton sweater and the newest designer jeans. She's just finished her callback and asks if I wanted to go over the scenes with her. I nod yes, feeling at once intimidated and stylishly deficient in my plain overalls. She sits down next to me and proceeds to give me direction on the scenes. Her direction is entirely different from what I've prepared and what the script calls for. As she leaves, she whispers: "You should always do what the director says." Just then, the casting director calls my name. I push my purple glasses up on my nose and walk into the audition room. I'm nearly done performing the first scene when the director says those dreaded words: "That's all we need."

I buried this story until it resurfaced twenty years later in a hypnosis session in Los Angeles. Once the story crystallized clearly, I realized that she'd intentionally distracted me that day and ruined my concentration on purpose. Today I share the details of this cautionary tale at every audition workshop I teach. There's very little another actor (or parent) can say to you at any moment in the often toxic waiting room that will make you feel good about yourself. Be careful. Protect yourself. Show business can unfortunately be a nasty business at times. Leave early and bring a raincoat—metaphorically and literally.

Leave Early

Auditions are stressful and often last minute. Yes, there may be times when you get a call in the morning from your agent asking you to show up in an hour for a shampoo commercial. You can't control your given appointment time, the audition location, congested traffic, a slow subway train, or a long wait in the crowded waiting room. And once you're in the audition room, you can't control the director, who may be eating sushi or texting during your audition. There are a few things you *can* control: arriving to the audition early (ideally ten minutes before your scheduled time) and being as prepared as possible.

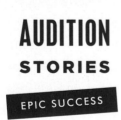

AUDITION STORIES

EPIC SUCCESS

The audition for Broadway's *Billy Elliot the Musical* was only my third audition, so I didn't have much experience. For the audition, we were asked to sing a song in our head voice. I decided for some reason to sing "Chitty Chitty Bang Bang," which is about as opposite to a pretty head voice song as you can get. Every single girl was singing "Castle on a Cloud" from *Les Mis*. I'm not exaggerating. I sang and belted my little heart out, smiling throughout the full song. While I was singing, one person started stamping their foot, and another started giggling. By the end of the song, the one that had been giggling was laughing so hard that he fell out of his chair. Someone had to help him up. I was so excited because I knew that it must have meant something! I have no idea what possessed me to sing that song, but it ended up working in my favor. Later that day, I got another callback, and a few months later, I was offered the role.

—IZZY HANSON-JOHNSTON,
age fifteen,
www.izzyhansonjohnston.com

Schedule Backward

Just as we made a budget in chapter 1, I also suggest making a schedule for the twenty-four hours leading up to the audition.

Here are some issues to consider when making your schedule:

- How will you get to the audition?

- What plans/meetings/work shifts do you need to reschedule in order to attend the audition?

- If you have children, do you have someone to look after them during the audition time?

- What time should you leave your home or job so that you arrive ten or fifteen minutes in advance of your scheduled audition time?

- Do you need to schedule sessions with your audition coach, acting teacher, or vocal coach to go over the audition material?

- Check the weather report. If you need to wear your red Hunter rain boots, plan to carry an attractive bag to hold your audition shoes.

- Figure out necessary hair and wardrobe issues. You'll need to plan ahead in terms of your appearance. To look your best, it's important to handle any dry cleaning, laundry, or ironing prior to the audition day.

Sounds exhausting, right? Perhaps at first. But learning to schedule your time will help you manage your audition needs, and you may start to see benefits in the rest of your life. Your number one priority is to do everything you can to be as prepared as possible for any audition in any circumstances.

Bring a Raincoat

My passion is long-distance cycling. In 1996 I rode my bike for four days and 375 miles from Boston to New York to raise money for AIDS research. There was a torrential storm on day three in rural Connecticut. I'd forgotten to pack rain gear, so I had to ride more than eighty miles wearing a trash bag over sopping wet cycling clothes. The following year, I did the ride again and packed my raincoat. The weather was perfect.

Moral of the story? Don't get caught in an unexpected storm. Bring your metaphorical raincoat with you to every audition by being as prepared as possible. Protect yourself against the audition elements.

AUDITION
STORIES

The Audition That Changed My Life

In the summer of 1997, I was doing community theater in Connecticut and I decided to try my luck at the open calls at the professional theaters in the area. The first one, at Hartford Stage, was a bust. But a week later I tried out a new monologue for the audition at Long Wharf Theatre in New Haven, and suddenly it all clicked. The next day I had a callback for the new artistic director, Doug Hughes, and he cast me in my professional debut, *She Stoops to Conquer*, and three other shows that season. So in one audition, I got four great credits and my Equity card. And fifteen years later, I made my Broadway debut in *An Enemy of the People*, directed by the very same Doug Hughes.

—MIKE BOLAND

— AUDITION DOS AND DON'TS —

- DO create a "portable office" in the car. Include extra snacks, water, clipboards, pens, pencils, highlighters, extra head shots, résumés, a hair brush, and bobby pins. If you're a stage mom, keep the backseat as a clean and organized space for your child to spread out and do homework in the car. Great way to multitask during traffic.

- If you arrive early, DO use the extra minutes to do final vocal warm-ups and any extra primping in your car. You want to look your best for your audition. As a rule, my mother never left the house without her lipstick applied, just in case she ran into Paul Newman at the supermarket. So go ahead and apply a little gloss in your rearview mirror in honor of my mother (and Mr. Newman).

- 👍 DO keep an extra outfit for you (and your child) in case one of you unexpectedly spills a snack or gets carsick in the Lincoln Tunnel.

- 👍 DO research the people who are in the audition room. Use Google or www.imbd.com to look up résumés and credits of industry professionals.

- 👍 DO carry a set of earbuds or noise-canceling headphones in case the waiting room gets loud.

- 👍 DO learn the script the way it is written. Don't paraphrase or add in any extra words. It's insulting to the writer, especially if they're in the audition room. Remember that the writer toiled for months to craft a script that the network and producers signed off on. The last thing anyone wants is for you to come in and rewrite.

- 👍 DO make the acting adjustment if the casting director or director suggests one. This means we like you and want to see if you can do it a different way. We need to see that you have the skills to think quickly and make changes on the spot. If you can't do this in the audition, then you certainly won't be able to in rehearsal or on the set.

- 👍 DO practice reading aloud every day so that you can be on your game if the casting director asks you to read a different scene on the spot.

- 👍 DO be prepared to stay. The casting director may ask you (or your child) to read for an additional part. Be flexible. Good thing you are reading aloud every day, as mentioned above.

- 👍 DO remember that the waiting room, elevator, and bathroom are public spaces. Save gossip and any postaudition meltdown for Starbucks or after-hours drinks with friends.

- 👎 DON'T vocalize in the waiting room or in the stairwell.

- 👎 DON'T apply your makeup, hair spray, or perfume in the public waiting room. Someone next to you might take offense, claiming that they're sensitive to smells. Avoid these awkward situations and touch up makeup in the privacy of your home, your car, or the restroom.

- 👎 DON'T be nosy and try to read the names of the actors who signed in on the sign-in sheet. It can make others feel uncomfortable if you're stalking the list, and it's really none of your business.

- 👎 DON'T expect to find extra time to run lines in the waiting room. Casting may be running ahead of schedule.

- 👎 DON'T tell us you're sick, contagious, or have a miserable cold. Sometimes the best auditions are the ones when you don't feel your best but somehow tap into a magical energy from deep inside.

- 👎 DON'T shake hands in the audition room unless someone from the creative team offers to first. I've gotten the stomach flu a few too many times after a long day of auditioning kids.

- 👎 DON'T be that actor who once auditioned for me and gushed how much he loved *Shrek*. If he'd done his homework and actually looked me up, he'd know I'd worked for Disney Animation, not DreamWorks.

- 👎 DON'T wear a costume to an audition unless requested to. I'll never forget the girl who came to an open call in Texas for *The Little Mermaid* on Broadway dressed in a shimmery blue mermaid dress. It's better to wear something that merely suggests the character. Use your good judgment. If the play takes place in the 1940s, wear a skirt and blouse, not your skinny jeans and Jimmy Choos.

"You're Wearing *That*?": What to Wear

Over the years my clothing style changed from preppy, to punk, to hippie, to grunge, to all black, and back again. My mother would often look at my outfits when I was on my way out the door and mutter: "You're wearing *that*? Well, it's a look."

Make my mother happy. You should have a few go-to audition outfits that work. Everyone's color palette will differ, depending on your particular skin tone and hair and eye color. Choose colors that make your eyes pop. You can get your colors "done" by a professional stylist or costume designer. Or just experiment and take a few photos in various outfits to determine which colors suit you best. Aim to have a few outfits that you love. Stick with these and then rotate out depending on the season or style trends.

AUDITION STORIES

EPIC FAIL

I will never forget my *Annie* callback for the 2012 Broadway revival. I was so pumped and excited to go in. When I did go in, I nailed my song, but from there, it all went downhill. They asked me to belt the ending of the song, but it was outside of my belting range. I cracked at least five times and I was totally humiliated. Then, they asked me to read Daddy Warbucks's lines, which totally took me off guard. I walked out of the room and did not feel good about myself. I felt like they made a fool of me.

—ANONYMOUS,
age fourteen

Preparing the Audition Material

The most important resource an actor has for rehearsing a part is audition sides. Sides are unique pages taken out of a script in order to help the actor prepare for the audition. They are usually sent by the casting office to the actor or to his/her representative, or made available online at www.sidesexpress.com.

If you get only the audition sides for a part from your agent, ask if there's a copy of the full script available. Sometimes we're allowed to release the full script; other times we can't. It varies from project to project. If it's a published play, get a copy from a bookstore or your local library and read through it.

I've been in the audition room too many times when an actor walks in and says: "I just got the material last night. I didn't have a chance to finish the play but I liked the few pages that I managed to read." Lovely. You've just admitted to the audition room that you're not only unprepared but inconsiderate as well. You've insulted the playwright because you clearly didn't take the time to read their play.

Prepare the scenes that are required in the order they are listed. Follow all directions. Do scene 1 first, then scene 2. Don't tell us that you want to start with scene 2. This is a huge red flag. The scenes are chosen in order of how we'd like to hear them—usually they progress in terms of emotions and story arc. They're numbered in a specific order for a reason.

Try to memorize the scenes. It's so refreshing when an actor knows the material off-book. But even if you've learned the scenes, do bring the script into the audition room with you. This shows us that you are not bound to your initial interpretation and are malleable and directable. Avoid reading lines from any electronic devices. Print your script pages. Invest in an affordable printer/scanner.

An Audition Is Not an Acting Class

The easiest way to break down an audition scene is to ask some basic questions and then make clear acting choices.

- What's the problem in the scene?

- What's the solution?

- What does my character want?

- What does the grammar and punctuation say?

The writer has toiled to perfect the audition scenes, so respect the script and use the scene as a road map to guide your audition. Make a choice with your scenes. Remember, it's just an audition, not life or death.

The Politics of the Waiting Room

When you arrive in the waiting room, sign in with the monitor so we know you're here, then find a seat. Since you're a professional actor, think of each audition as a job interview. You have only one chance to make a good first impression. To stay focused and in the zone, consider wearing headphones and listening to quiet music. Leave your day behind you when you walk into the casting office. Be conscious of how you interact with the monitors and casting staff in the waiting room. If you're considerate and kind, my assistant will mention it to me and help you move forward. Conversely, if you act like a jerk, she'll tell me that, too. Because she's a good assistant, she won't want her boss to look like an idiot because of you.

There is nothing another actor can say to you in the waiting room that will make you feel good in that moment. We are by nature social, creative, and chatty people. I'm not insisting that you take an oath of silence in the waiting room. But be aware of your behavior. Be considerate of other people. Treat other people the way you would like to be treated. You may not think you're distracting other actors, but when you chat them up, you're subconsciously shifting their focus away from their audition material and killing their concentration.

Of course, no one's perfect. All the scheduling and preparation you've done in advance can fall apart in an instant if traffic comes to a sudden standstill, your train breaks down, or you suddenly develop a migraine. The key is to try your best to arrive with your life together. But we're all human. Things happen. If today's audition didn't go well, there will always be another one.

Is Our Table Ready Yet?

The audition waiting room is just like hostessing at a restaurant. In both settings people are constantly coming up to you asking when it's going to be their turn to be seated or their turn to be seen.

—MEGHAN FLAIM,
2013 summer intern for
Jen Rudin Casting

Flying In for Auditions

Unless you work for an airline, it takes time, effort, and money to fly to a major city for an audition. Choose wisely when deciding to spend money on a flight. Is it your dream role? Did you send in a tape and get called to a larger city for a callback? If so, go ahead: cash in those miles and book a flight. If you are flying in, avoid flying the same day as the audition or taking a red-eye flight the night before. Too much can go wrong. Better to land the day before the audition so you can get up the next day and hit the ground running.

Leave Your Baggage at the Door

Over the years, I've seen actors come into the audition with all kinds of baggage, both physical and emotional. One of the best things you can to do to prepare for an audition is to be as organized as possible. Leave the messy binders and overflowing tote bags outside. No one wants to hear about the delays on the FDR or the weird man who meowed at you on the subway. We all traveled to get to the audition. Smile and do your best. Then pick up your bags at baggage claim and get on with your day.

Have a Cup of Coffee and Find Your Personality

I've often had important meetings scheduled for later in the afternoon—not at all my ideal time of day. When an afternoon meeting confirms, I always follow my mother's advice: "Have a cup of coffee and find your personality." Whether that means a literal cup of coffee just before the meeting, a Snickers bar, or running in place on the sidewalk to get your adrenaline going, figure out what you need to do to arrive at your scheduled appointment time with your personality intact. Whatever else happened that day, leave it at the door and walk into your audition with a positive attitude, a big smile, and a whole lot of confidence!

JEN'S LAST WORD

> The casting director's job is to help you get the job. Do a great audition. Then leave the room, forget about the audition, put on your raincoat, and get on with the rest of your day. If you've done the best you can, the rest is out of your hands.

CHAPTER FOUR

PILOT SEASON PANIC

AUDITIONING FOR TV AND FILM

t's 1985 and I'm at the final callback for an ABC series called *Growing Pains*. They're looking to replace the actress who played Carol Seaver in the pilot episode. My starting salary's been negotiated at $5,000 an episode. If I get the role, my mother and I will move to Los Angeles and my father will stay in New York with my sister, Eve. At the final hour, Tracey Gold gets the role. She's already done the series *Goodnight, Beantown* and has many more TV credits than me. I'm crushed when I don't get the part, but I force myself to watch the show each week for the next seven years.

Initial Research for Film and TV Auditions

If you're interested in pursuing television and film roles—and what actor isn't?—your first step is to start watching a lot of TV and going to the movies.

Have an informed opinion about your favorite actors and why you like their work. Think about your favorite current long-running shows on television. We're consistently loyal to the shows we love and we root for the actors every week in our living room. We're mesmerized by their story arcs. We feel like they're our friends.

Thanks to technology, we can watch media on all our devices. I subscribe to Hulu Plus and Netflix, and enjoy watching my favorite shows from the various networks' apps anytime on my iPad. I also DVR every new show at least once to check out the actors and stories, then make decisions on which shows I will watch regularly. Do your research. I cannot overstate the importance of this!

Single-Camera Comedy versus Multicamera Comedy

When preparing for a TV audition, know the type of show you're auditioning for. The information can be found on the casting breakdown or by asking your agent or the casting office. A one-hour drama (*The West Wing, Grey's Anatomy*) differs from a half-hour comedy (*Modern Family, Two and a Half Men*). Some half hours are multicamera (*Cheers, Friends*). Some are single camera (*30 Rock, The Office*). Feature films are often produced by studios (Warner Bros., New Line, 20th Century Fox), but sometimes are independently produced. Know the kind of TV show or film you are auditioning for.

In a single-camera comedy, each shot is filmed individually. For a *30 Rock* scene that cuts back and forth between Liz Lemon and Tracy Jordan, the camera will shoot Tina Fey's lines separately from Tracy Morgan's, and then the shots will be edited together later into a single scene.

Multicamera comedies do things the "old-timey" way. Sometimes they are filmed in front of a live studio audience, with few interruptions, while a handful of cameras tape the action. Often there's a laugh track and a familiar setup/punch line formula.

**AUDITION
STORIES**

The Audition That Changed My Life

The audition that changed my life was for the ABC TV series *The Neighbors*. I auditioned for it and didn't hear anything for a bit. But then, they called me out to California for a screen test! I was so excited! It was my first screen test and my first time in California. It took a few days, which felt like forever, but I finally got the call: my agent telling me I got the part! Sadly, after the table read they decided that I looked too much older than the boy playing opposite me, so they had to let me go. Though not a great outcome, I was able to see the bright side of the experience. I finally got to do a screen test for ABC, I made it to California, and best of all, I have kept in touch with the writer of the show, who was always very supportive of me and is a really great guy. The situation was a good learning experience in how to handle the disappointments that can come in this business.

—TYLER BACKER,
age eleven

Camera Framing for TV and Film Auditions

When you audition for TV or film, the camera frames you from the shoulders up. Imagine a small box around your face. That's your camera frame. Because it is so close, the camera sees and picks up everything you do. The camera either likes you or it doesn't. Some actors look great, while others fall into the "camera adds ten pounds" category.

Take an on-camera class that meets for a few weeks so you can get used to coming in and working. If you're brilliant one week, you may not be the next. It's important to assess what works for you and what doesn't. When I teach on-camera classes, I always e-mail actors their clips so they can see how they look on camera and watch their progression as the class goes on. You won't know what you look like or what habitual tics you display on camera until you see yourself on tape. You must do this in advance of coming in for your real audition. An audition is not the place to experiment with new acting styles or TV acting techniques. Work all that out in a good on-camera class ahead of time so you are ready to come in and focus on giving a great audition. Check my website (www.jenrudin.com) to find out more about my on-camera classes and workshops.

ASK THE ACTOR

What's the difference between acting onstage versus acting for film and TV?

Onstage, you have to project your voice and make sure the people in the last row experience your performance. On TV, if I raise my eyebrow and they add in some underscoring music, I've just had an acting moment.

—DENNIS BOUTSIKARIS

AGENT'S CORNER

What words come to mind to describe pilot season?

Hell. Agony. Insanity. Exciting. Grueling. Frenzied. Barbaric. High-energy. Fast-paced. Hectic. Long hours. A mad scramble. High intensity. Pressured. Exhausting. Stress. Survival of the fittest. Organized chaos. Anything can happen.

Pilot Season

Pilot season. Two words that make casting directors, agents, managers, and actors go immediately into overdrive.

Each summer, the major American broadcast television networks receive about five hundred brief elevator pitches for new shows from writers and producers. In the fall, each network requests scripts for about seventy pitches and, the following January, orders about twenty pilot episodes. Actors come to Los Angeles from all over the United States and around the world to audition for them between January and March. By spring, actors are cast and production crews assembled to produce the pilots.

Network pilots (CBS, NBC, ABC) are shot in March and April. Then, in May, at the upfronts,* the networks announce which pilots they will be picking up to turn into series and which of the shows already on the air they are renewing. Cable networks produce pilots year round, so the same timeline does not apply to them.

Welcome to pilot season!

Getting cast in a television pilot is one of the most stressful and exciting experiences for the actor, the agent, and the casting director, though it can often be heartbreaking as well. There's a huge committee of people deciding your fate and a lot of money at stake.

Pilot season is, in a word, thrilling. The busy and hectic pace makes for long hours for everyone. Often the race is on to make offers to "names"

---

* In the North American television industry, an *upfront* is a meeting hosted at the start of important advertising sales periods by television network executives, attended by the press and major advertisers. It allows marketers to buy television commercial airtime "up front," or several months before the television season begins.

(recognized actors or other celebrities), but then we must have backup choices if the name actor passes. Roles often change gender, ethnicity, and age, sometimes right in the middle of a casting session. Casting actors for a pilot is a crazy mix of timing, availability, and talent. There's no formula, and every pilot season has different casting trends. Patience and flexibility are key. We don't always know who is right for the role. Then, when we least expect it, an actor will come in and bring the character to life. It takes only one actor, but the search can sometimes feel endless.

Don't Be That Obnoxious Film Guy

In the middle of a hectic day of pilot season auditions, an actor was about to start his first audition scene. I said: "The pacing of this show is very much like *The West Wing*." He interrupted me: "I don't watch TV. I'm more of a film actor." Really? That's nice. But this is a TV audition. All prepared actors should understand contemporary TV references. Ditto for film. Your job is to watch TV and films. Do your homework. Become an expert on the genres. Don't be pretentious, be educated. Next, please.

Getting into the Room

In order to get seen for a pilot, your first step as an actor is to get into the room for an audition. This does not happen overnight. An actor must have relationships with casting directors. Be smart and do your networking in the fall, in advance of pilot season, and keep in touch with the people you've made connections with as pilot season draws near. Pilot season is hardly the time for me to meet new actors, unless I'm trying to cast a children's role or doing a focused search for a specific ethnicity.

Hopefully your agent will submit you and I'll give them an appointment time for you. Then it's up to you to prepare!

From behind the camera taping actress Penny McNamee during pilot season, 2013.

Respect the Punctuation in the Script

By the time you get the audition scenes, the writer has perfected the script and then gotten approval on the scenes from the network and studio. The script is your road map. Use it to guide you. Respect the words.

Following is a sample script from a pilot. I've circled punctuation. If there's an exclamation point, the writer put it there for a reason. Same with ellipses and question marks. I have also highlighted the character's lines and actions. Take a look.

Broadcaster? Casting Director? Creative team?

CRASH & BERNSTEIN Pilot

"Cleo"

Scene Slug *What's the problem?*

WYATT HEADS FOR THE DOOR, CLEARLY IN A RUSH. CLEO STOPS HIM.

↳ Action!

Strut

Solution?

Wyatt's sister. she is "the artist". Sensitive and emotional. Heightened sense of drama...

> CLEO *II*
>
> Wyatt, can I ask you a quick question?
>
> WYATT
>
> Uh, I'm kinda in a hurry, but sure.
>
> CLEO *UHT JHT*
>
> Okay, well there's this boy in my
> talented and gifted class, and he's
> kind of cute — I mean, not like (MOCK
> AWE) 'Ahh! You're so gorgeous I
> forgot how to chew my food' cute, but
> definitely like a (SINGS) 'Here comes
> a cute boy' level of cuteness.
> Anyway, I wrote him a haiku, and--
>
> WYATT
>
> I thought you said it was a quick
> question.
>
> CLEO *III*
>
> You know what, this is silly. You're
> not going to know the answer anyway.
>
> WYATT
>
> Great, then I guess I'll just see you--
>
> CLEO *I*
>
> We should role play!
>
> WYATT
>
> What? No. Cleo, I really need to--

1/3

Being an Audition Reader at a Casting Session

I often use actors whom I know and trust as audition readers in my auditions. They are usually actors I've auditioned over the years who have become acquaintances or friends. It's great for the actor who's auditioning, because they have a scene partner to feed them the other lines in the scene. For the actors who are audition readers, it's a great way to get to know a casting director, and you get to spend the day watching other actors' auditions. Many aspects of the audition process get demystified, in the best possible way. Many tell me that spending a few hours as an audition reader is like taking a master class in audition technique.

Here's what some of my audition readers had to say after spending time as my reader during pilot season:

> Being a reader for Jen helped me learn about the importance of quick pacing in television auditions, simple outfit choices, and that not everything has to be small and introverted—especially for comedy. There is a fine line between being fun and conversational and taking up too much of the casting director's time, and it's extremely important to be aware of that. Jen would point out when people looked right for the part—they wore a blazer or they did their hair differently than usual—and how it really worked for the role for which they were auditioning. She also pointed out what didn't work—hair and makeup should be simple, and too many accessories can be distracting. One of the most important things I learned is to *stay close to the script*. It's appropriate to maybe add a bit of your own flair at the end of a scene, but *don't mess around with the writing*. One person was very funny and had great comedic timing, but Jen couldn't send her tape in because she wasn't sticking to the script at all. The

writer wrote those words for a reason, and he or she wants to hear you say them.

—BECKY CHICOINE,
www.beckychicoine.com

An actor came in to read for a role. He looked great, he was lovely in the room, and he was clearly talented. However, his face was stuck in his sides during the audition. Jen gave him direction. He wasn't able to take it because he was relying on the sides for his lines. When he left the room, Jen said how disappointed she was. She couldn't post his tape, because his face was buried in his page. If he had been more prepared his tape would have been posted, and he would have had the opportunity to get called back. In that moment I learned a very valuable lesson. Even though it seems obvious, *it is essential that you come into the room completely prepared with your material*. It is literally the least you can do, and it may be the difference between getting a callback and then booking a job or not making it past your initial audition.

—FELICIA BLUM,
www.feliciablum.weebly.com

You hear it all the time, but I really saw firsthand that so much of the casting process really IS out of our hands. So instead of worrying about "what they are looking for," just do your job: bring the character to life! I never expected that Jen would ask me to audition for one of her projects, but she did, and that audition led to a callback for a series regular in an ABC pilot. Just goes to show, you never know!

—HALLE MORSE,
www.hallemorse.com

AUDITION
STORIES

The Audition That Changed My Life

The audition that changed my life was for the film *Exorcist III*. I was in high school and it was filming in my hometown of Wilmington, North Carolina. I had very little experience in any kind of acting and especially in film. I decided to go down to the casting office one afternoon and drop off a "head shot" (a Polaroid my mom had taken in the front yard) and try to get someone to hire me as an extra. After getting up the courage to go into the office, I made small talk with the receptionist, dropped off my picture, and turned to leave when I heard a voice from above me say, "What's your name?" I thought he wasn't talking to me, so I walked out of the office. Two minutes later the receptionist came running out and said that the director, William Peter Blatty, was the person calling me and he wanted to talk to me. I went back in, apologizing profusely. We spoke briefly and they gave me an audition for the next day. It was three lines, and I was so thrilled. I came back and read for him the next day and then didn't hear anything for about a month. I was waiting tables for the summer when I got a call from casting saying that I had been hired. I showed up on set and went directly to the area marked as "Extras Holding," assuming I had been hired as an extra. I had been there about twenty minutes when I heard the radios buzzing that they were looking for a missing actor named . . . Manley Pope! "Um, I'm Manley Pope," I said to the PA, and they whisked me away to my own tiny shared honey wagon* trailer with my name written in Sharpie on the door. I had been booked as a day player for the week . . . with lines!!! From this one job I got my SAG card, worked in a scene with George C. Scott, and made fifteen hundred dollars. And the next day, I finally quit my job waiting tables.

—MANLEY POPE

After Your Audition

I will take a strong position when I think an actor's really right for a role. If the pilot's writers and producers like the audition, we see if we can get it to the next step, which is a test deal. When this happens, the agent negotiates the terms of the contract in advance with a business and legal affairs representative from the studio or network. When the deal is closed, the actor (and parent, if it's a young actor) will be flown to L.A. to test at the studio in front of a bunch of executives. If they are "approved" by the studio, the next step is to test in front of the network that same afternoon or the next day. This can be a life-changing twenty-four hours for the actor and the agent, or it can be very disappointing. Either way, testing for a pilot is a huge deal.

When pilot season's over, I often contract bronchitis from pure exhaustion. Or take long naps for a few days following the madness. If an actor did not book a pilot, this is also a good time for them to take that much-needed vacation to relax and recharge.

---

* A *honey wagon* is a type of multiroom trailer used by film and television productions.

AUDITION
STORIES

EPIC FAIL

You never want to walk into an audition room and see a man behind the table that you broke up with the week before. This is why I don't date in the industry! I went to an audition for a new Broadway musical, not knowing that a guy I dumped was the producer. As soon as I walked in and saw him, my stomach dropped and I knew then and there I wasn't going to get the part. I wanted so badly to just thank them and leave, but I sang and read my sides and as I suspected, didn't get a callback. Moral of the story: DON'T SHIT WHERE YOU EAT!

—RENA STROBER,
www.renastrober.com

TV AND FILM AUDITION
—— DOS AND DON'TS ——

- 🖓 DON'T come into the audition room and demand to sit if you're asked to stand. Follow simple directions. My associate Bess Fifer sums it up perfectly: "If you were at someone's house for a dinner party, would you walk in and immediately rearrange the furniture?"

- 🖓 DON'T ask if you can walk into the scene or walk out of the scene. We're not shooting a movie, just trying to get you the job.

- 🖓 DON'T come in with too many props. This can work for a theater audition but not for film and TV. I've had actors insist on eating food, which ends up leaving crumbs on the floor and a lingering stinky smell in the room. Not cool.

🖐 DON'T stage your audition scene. This is not a theater rehearsal. The camera frames you close up. For now, keep it simple and make a great audition tape. I'm not a director of photography, and there's limited framing with the cameras we use for auditions.

🖐 DON'T change the order of the scenes. Always perform them in the order they were given to you.

🖐 DON'T argue. If you're given a note, take it and make the adjustment.

🖐 DON'T come in unprepared. You must memorize your scenes, or at least be as "off-book" as possible. Why? Because the camera is on you and we want to see your eyes and a full performance. The moment you look down to your script, you've dropped out of the scene and we've lost you. It's hard enough to get your tape watched by the L.A. casting directors and producers. You've got to know your lines, otherwise you've already blown your chance.

🖐 DON'T forget to staple your photo to your résumé. Even if I have a stapler close by, why waste two minutes talking about how you didn't staple your picture and résumé together when we could have been discussing the scene?

👍 DO come in prepared with your scenes—ideally, have them memorized.

👍 DO download an iPhone app such as LineLearner, Rehearsal, or Scene Study to help memorize scripts.

👍 DO bring your script into the room with you. Even if you hold it in your hands, you want to show us that you're flexible and not a fully finished product. Show us that you're malleable and open to direction.

👍 DO listen and think. You should always be listening to the other person in the scene and thinking about something, even if it's your shopping list or what you're going to cook for dinner.

👍 DO know your colors and what works for your skin tone.

👍 DO come in wearing a solid color for the camera. Most backdrops are blue or gray and you will be filmed in front of them, so that should help when choosing your wardrobe. Find your go-to audition outfit and keep wearing it! Last pilot season two women wore the same blue dress from Brooklyn Industries. The blue made their eyes pop. I liked the dress so much I bought the same one a few days later.

👍 DO apply basic makeup if you're a woman. Eyes tend to look beady or small if you skip the eyeliner or mascara. Remember your framing: from the shoulders up, and maybe closer. You don't want to come in with theatrical makeup on, but you also don't want to be washed out. My mother always said, "Just a little lipstick, please," and she's right. If you need advice, visit a MAC store or the makeup counter at Bloomingdale's, or watch a YouTube video on how to apply makeup.

👍 DO your hair. Spend the money on a professional blowout if it's right for your character. You can shop around to find a decent price for a quick blow-dry. It makes a big difference. And consider a curling wand. Ricky's sells them. Throw it in your bag, plug it in for a quick touch-up, and you're set.

👍 DO steam or iron your clothing. Remember, any audition is a job interview, so you want to make sure you look your best. Last I checked, a steam iron was under $30 at any drugstore.

JEN'S LAST WORD

" You have one chance to make a good first impression. This applies to most things in life, but it's especially true during pilot season. Make a great first impression, and I'll keep bringing you in to audition. Maybe one day you'll get lucky and get your big break in a show like *Growing Pains*!

CHAPTER FIVE

SOMEDAY I'LL BE PART OF YOUR WORLD

AUDITIONING FOR BROADWAY AND THEATER

For my ninth birthday, my parents give me the *Annie* original cast album. I spend hours after school every day blasting the record on my parents' stereo, mouthing the words to "Tomorrow" in front of their bedroom mirror. No wonder my sister ignores me to read comic books and watch *The Bionic Woman*. I write a letter to the Broadway theater where *Annie* is playing and ask them to please contact me the next time there's an audition. I'm so obsessed with the show that in fifth grade, I adapt, produce, cast, and direct my own production starring yours truly in the title role. My stuffed bulldog Boubi plays Sandy. We run for two performances in front of the entire school and everyone's parents.

That production of *Annie* taught me a few lessons. Number one: your friends will definitely stop speaking to you when you fire them (like I did) and decide to recast for creative reasons. Number two: I actually can't really sing.

But don't despair, dear reader. What I lacked in vocal range, I sure made up for in ego.

Disney on Broadway

I often joke that it's easier to book a role on a television show then it is to get cast in a Broadway show. Actors are required not only to sing, act, *and* dance (thus, the expression *triple threat*), but also to prove they possess the stamina to perform eight times a week. Musical theater auditions take place in numerous sessions over a period of time, sometimes encompassing six months or even several years. Actors may audition multiple times for a Broadway show and still end up getting cut from the audition or kept in the DTL ("down the line") files for later. Sometimes a role will become available and you will get cast years after your first audition. As with most auditions in this business, timing and patience are key.

During my time as director of casting and talent development at the Walt Disney Company, I was charged by Disney Theatrical Productions president Thomas Schumacher to unify the talent across all the Disney Broadway shows and tours and to focus specifically on children's casting for *Mary Poppins*, *The Lion King*, and *The Little Mermaid*. I conducted open calls* across the country for the highly coveted roles of Jane and Michael Banks in *Mary Poppins* and Ariel in *The Little Mermaid*. Before I'd leave for a talent search, my boss would remind me that I was the public face of the Walt Disney Company, and that I should make sure that everyone had a positive experience at the audition. I aspired to practice kindness and hoped for no tears.

Easier said than done. At a children's open call for *Mary Poppins* in Atlanta, fifty children stood in a semicircle. Each child wore a "Hello, My Name Is" name tag, with a number written on it instead of their name. I jotted numbers down for the ones I'd ask to stay. By this point, the show had been on Broadway for over a year, so we had very clear ideas on the age, height, and look for Jane and Michael Banks. After I made my way around the circle, the excited children waited for me to read the numbers for who would stay to work on scenes and music.

Reading the numbers in the casting elimination process is always a dramatic moment in the open call process. I read ten numbers. When I was finished, a freckled redheaded girl burst into loud, hysterical sobs because her

---

* An *open call* is an audition that is open to anyone who shows up.

number had not been called. I was shocked. We quickly found her mother in the waiting room and she took her sobbing daughter home. I felt bad for making her cry, but just because you cry doesn't mean you get to stay.

The image of that crying girl in Atlanta stayed with me. From then on, at all future open calls, I always called the parents into the room just before I made the cuts. I would announce that I was cutting a number of the children because they might be too tall or too short or just not quite the right look for Victorian England. And though at that moment their child may not quite be ready for Broadway, I urged everyone to feel encouraged by this audition process and continue to study voice, dance, and acting.

Big Stars' Big Breaks

While I was a casting executive at the Walt Disney Studios, we cast many young people in their first feature films: Anne Hathaway, Lindsay Lohan, Amy Adams, Abigail Breslin, Kellan Lutz, Joseph Gordon Levitt, Anna Faris, Chris Pine, Rachel McAdams, Megan Fox, Jennifer Garner, and Heath Ledger, to name a few.

Perhaps one of the most memorable audition processes for me was when Rachel McAdams auditioned for Rob Schneider's *Hot Chick*. She lived in Toronto and had recently graduated from theater school. She had also skated competitively. She was put on tape by the local CD and it was my job to view the tapes. I was immediately drawn to her reading. Even on a crappy tape she shined. She was prepared, honest, and in the moment, and she had a natural charm and charisma that were immediately captivating. We flew her to L.A. to audition for us, and she exuded natural grace and confidence despite the fact that she had just gotten off a plane. She never lagged during the entire process. We had her read a number of scenes, finally culminating with having to be Rob Schneider in a woman's body doing a pole dance. She had to play two characters in this movie and be pretty outrageous, but Rachel went for it without any hesitation or self-consciousness. Rob Schneider was bowled over. During the screen test, her physicality, humor, and sheer fearlessness were awe inspiring. She didn't shrink or judge herself in what was a pretty silly, albeit fun concept. She also had a great time playing this role of the "hot chick." I believe competing in skating coupled with her theater training had prepared her for this experience.

For the second *Princess Diaries*, we had to find a suitable prince for Anne Hathaway. He had to be charming, handsome, likable, and able to do physical comedy. We saw many actors for the part and were shocked at how many hadn't even bothered to see the first *Princess Diaries* movie. My colleague Marcia Ross and I read a young man who had worked at the Williamstown Theatre Festival the summer before. He embodied all the qualities we were looking for and had an ease and modesty about him despite his charm and good looks. He also had the acting chops, having trained and performed quite a bit onstage. We couldn't wait to introduce this young man to Garry Marshall. His name was Chris Pine.

The young actor who most embodied confidence, charisma, and a complete lack of fear was young Heath Ledger. At nineteen, he was already somewhat of a star in Australia. He was completely prepared, and he owned the room. His natural exuberance and charm were overpowering. Gil Junger, our director, remarked afterward that he would have wanted to be Heath Ledger in high school. Heath was also completely engaging and friendly. He seemed to be in on a cosmic joke and had an air of mystery about him. We all couldn't help but be won over by both his performance and his personality. He didn't display any self-consciousness or self-doubt. After seeing him read and test, we knew he was destined for great things.

All of these actors were fearless and had fun. They owned the audition process while they were there. They were prepared but could also be spontaneous, and they all put the filmmakers at ease with their confidence that they could play the part. They executed their ideas without self-consciousness or self-doubt.

—DONNA MORONG,
*casting director and co-owner of
Aquila Morong Studio in Los Angeles
(www.aquilamorongstudio.com)*

The $110 Ticket

At Disney Theatrical Productions, we'd narrow down our casting choices, then ask ourselves: "Does this actor give me a performance worth the $110 ticket price? Will the actor's performance communicate clearly to the folks in the last row in the balcony?" If someone in the audience is blind or deaf, they should still be able to enjoy your performance. The stakes are high. You'd better be able to hit that high note every night, eight performances a week, or someone will want their money back. When a theatergoer adds in the costs of a babysitter, gas, parking, tolls, dinner, and dessert, going to see a Broadway show becomes one very expensive night. Our job is to make sure the experience is worth the cost by casting the right talent in every role, making it an unforgettable night for theatergoers.

AUDITION STORIES

EPIC FAIL

I was auditioning for a revival of *Gypsy* that would be directed by the legendary author-director Arthur Laurents, who was about ninety years old at the time. I was excited just to *meet* him, much less audition for him. I finished my audition and there was a *very* long pause as he looked at me and just sat thinking. I wondered if I was supposed to leave or not. Finally, he said, "I see what you're doing . . . but I don't want you to do it." Fortunately, he respected my choice enough that he gave me adjustments and let me try again!

—TONY FREEMAN

Open Calls for Broadway Shows and Tours

Every Broadway show is required by Actors Equity Association (AEA)* to conduct open calls once every six months. The audition information is listed on the AEA website, as well as www.playbill.com and www.backstage.com. The musical director (or someone from the music department) is required to attend the audition. AEA actors will be given priority for an appointment slot. If you're nonunion, stick around; you may get seen if there are available time slots left in the day. Getting seen depends on how many AEA actors show up. If you can't get seen but feel strongly that you're perfect for the show, keep an eye on the open call listings and keep coming back to the open calls. It may take several attempts, but hopefully you'll get seen at some point.

Once you get into the audition room, plan to sing either an up-tempo show song, a ballad from a show, or a pop/rock song. Choose a song that's right for the style of the show and is age appropriate for you. I've seen little boys sing "The Impossible Dream," from *Man of La Mancha*, and grown women sing "I Enjoy Being a Girl." The song should fit the show but also needs to fit you.

During a day of open calls, I usually make three piles of photos and résumés: yes, no, and maybe. Many actors end up in the no pile because,

---

* Actors' Equity Association (AEA) is the labor union representing American actors and stage managers in the theater. Check out http://www.actorsequity.org for more information.

despite their dreams, they're just not vocally strong enough for a Broadway show. If you end up in the yes pile or maybe pile, that means we'll keep you in the files for the future and will call you in for an appointment when a role opens up. Many actors have gotten cast in their first Broadway show from attending open calls, so do not give up!

AUDITION STORIES

EPIC SUCCESS

One of my first really big jobs was playing Val in the twenty-fifth-anniversary national tour of *A Chorus Line*. So when the Broadway revival was announced for 2006, I was very excited to see if I might somehow fit into that production. I went to the initial auditions and danced myself to death, but they were apparently on the fence as to where I fit in this time around. After my first audition, however, I unfortunately had to have knee surgery due to cartilage damage. Of course, just weeks after the surgery, my agents got a call that they were calling me back for *A Chorus Line* to possibly cover Cassie. There was to be no dancing at this audition, since I'd already proven myself there, but they wanted me to sing and read again.

Several people told me I was insane to even consider it, but I felt that I had earned that callback with a lot of blood, sweat, and tears. Also, the show didn't start rehearsals for months, so I learned the material and limped my way to the callback. On crutches! Even more than that, I had a brace on my leg from hip to ankle. And you know what? I sang and acted my face off. I pretty much knew I wouldn't get the part, but I showed them my tenacity and what I was made of.

Fast-forward two years. Lots of rehab later, I was finally in elite dancer shape again and I got another audition for the show. I went in and danced as if I had never been injured. Then I sang and read. And when I delivered the line "I haven't worked in two years, not really," as Cassie, the line had new meaning, because I had not worked in my real life due to complications from that knee surgery. Thanks to all that hard work, I landed a slot as a vacation swing covering Cassie and Sheila in the Broadway company of *A Chorus Line* (which eventually became a permanent standby position for me).

—KIMBERLY DAWN NEUMANN,
www.kdneumann.com

ASK THE VOCAL COACH

What is a musical theater audition binder, and what should a singer put in it?

Any standard three-ring binder can be used for your audition music. Preferably, your binder will have stiff covers so that it stays open on a music stand, and have a ring size of between 1 and 1½ inches. Whether you choose to use plastic page protectors or holes punched in heavy paper, it's important to make reading your music as easy as possible for the accompanist. Be sure to have the pages of music back to back, to minimize the number of page turns.

I also recommend using at least three different binders for music:

- A main one for current, performance-ready songs

- Another for songs you're working on

- One more to store music you'd like to learn eventually but are not planning on performing at present

The contents of the binders can be arranged in any order that makes sense to you and enables you to locate what you need quickly. Consider a contents page at the front of each of your binders to keep you organized and able to find a song quickly during an audition. Each song should be marked for sixteen- and thirty-two-bar cuts.

Songs in your main performance binder need to demonstrate your versatility in a variety of styles. These would include:

- Broadway up-tempos (fast songs)

- Ballads (slow songs) from both traditional and contemporary shows

- Any specialty types of songs that you're comfortable with, such as jazz, country, or classical. Nowadays, many auditions ask for non-Broadway pop, rock, or R&B (rhythm and blues) songs, so be sure to include one or two of those. In addition, a Disney-type song is also good to have prepared.

Finally, although all your music should be clearly marked for the pianist, you'll want at least one of your songs to be somewhat "pianist-proof" (for those times when you have doubts about the accompanist's ability to sight-read well).

—BOB MARKS,
vocal coach,
www.bobmarks.com

Preparing for a Broadway Audition

When you get an appointment for a Broadway show or tour audition, you'll be e-mailed the material in advance. It will likely include sheet music for a song or songs from the show and an audition scene. Go ahead and place the current audition material into your audition binder. You may be asked to bring dance clothing too. It's helpful to meet with a vocal coach or a voice teacher to help learn the songs. It's also a good idea to meet with an acting coach to go over the scene. Look at the punctuation. Make a list of what the character wants in the scene and note the obstacles in the scene. What is the problem and what's the solution? Most scenes can be broken down that simply.

Be prepared and you'll give a great audition.

AUDITION STORIES

The Audition That Changed My Life

The audition that changed my life was probably when I auditioned for the musical *How the Grinch Stole Christmas* for the third time. Every other time, I had gotten to the final callback but just missed getting cast. For the third time, I was at the final callback. I went through all the rounds of cuts and they even took measurements for costumes. I was sure I would get it this time! Later, I learned that I didn't get the role and was absolutely devastated. I was eight years old and I remember lying down in bed with my mom and crying about how I wasn't good enough and how I was never going to get anything. Really a life changer. At that moment, I thought my life was over, but I went on to do four national tours and then Broadway. The experience made me realize that it's all about timing.

—CAMILLE MANCUSO,
age thirteen,
www.camillemancuso.com

Making Mermaids Sing

In January 2009, I conducted a ten-city, two-week search for a replacement Ariel for *The Little Mermaid* on Broadway. I auditioned six hundred actresses, all of whom had dreams of playing Ariel. My first stop was Cincinnati. The auditions were held in a dingy hotel conference room. A freshman from the Cincinnati Conservatory of Music (CCM) volunteered to help out and accompanied the actresses as best he could on his keyboard. We were in a drab room with poor lighting, tepid air, and no real piano. All the girls who sang for me were mediocre. No one was ready for Broadway. I was feeling sleepy, and about to send one of the volunteers out to get me a double espresso when a junior at CCM named Megan Campanile walked in. Megan impressed me immediately. She was a petite redhead with a strong singing voice and many years of dance training and gymnastics. I uploaded her audition to the YouTube channel I'd created for Ariel casting. After my ten-city, two-week casting search, Megan was one of six actresses out of six hundred invited to attend the final callback in New York and ultimately got cast in her first Broadway show.

*With my mermaid,
Megan Campanile, at
the final performance of*
The Little Mermaid *on
Broadway, 2009.*
(JOE ABRAHAM)

We hired Megan to play one of Ariel's sisters and to cover the role of Ariel. At that moment in time, Megan was hirable for Broadway. Not only was she a triple threat (equally proficient in singing, dancing, and acting), she was also in the right place at the right time. As for the other 599 actresses who auditioned in cities such as Chicago, Dallas, Denver, Los Angeles, Boston, and Philadelphia, they either couldn't hit the necessary high E in "Part of Your World" or just didn't look right for the role. They simply weren't ready for Broadway.

Megan thanked me in her *Playbill* bio, calling me her "Jewish fairy godmother." We're still close today, bonded from that day when we met in Cincinnati and her life changed forever.

I once got really, really sick with a virus, but I was determined to go to this audition because I knew I was perfect for the role of a beauty pageant contestant from Poland. Despite the fact that I was very dizzy and could barely breathe, I was doing well. Until they asked me to do the sides again, this time with a Polish accent. I was completely caught off guard, and what came out of me was a mixture of all sorts of accents, primarily sounding more Chinese than Polish. The embarrassment must have caused my already high fever to go up a few degrees.

—ANNA LAKOMY

Under the Sea: Replacing Sebastian in *The Little Mermaid* on Broadway

"Under the Sea" is the showstopping song in the Broadway production of *The Little Mermaid*. Tituss Burgess had originated* the role on Broadway and often brought the house down when he hit those insanely high notes every show. When he left the show in order to play a lead role in the *Guys and Dolls* Broadway revival, he left very big shoes to fill.

We began a search in earnest for a replacement and engaged in weeks of auditions. We needed a performer with humor, vocal chops, and warmth. We saw every actor available at the time, but my boss, Thomas Schumacher, didn't sign off on any of our choices. So we continued the casting search.

---

* When an actor *originates* a role, it means that he or she is the first person to play that part in the original Broadway cast.

At the 2009 Broadway closing of The Little Mermaid *with Rogelio Douglas Jr., who starred as Sebastian, and my niece, Emma.*

That weekend, I took a group of campers from Stagedoor Manor to see a matinee performance of the Broadway musical *In the Heights*. It was my fifth time seeing the show, and at this particular rainy Saturday matinee, the actor playing Benny was out of the show, home recovering from a stomach bug he'd contracted on a recent vacation to Mexico. His understudy had recently left the show to star in a Broadway revival of *Godspell*, which had just been postponed. So that day, it was up to the swing actor,* Rogelio Douglas Jr., to perform the role of Benny. From the moment he first sang, I couldn't take my eyes off of him. I met him after the show, gave him my business card, and told him to call me on Monday.

We set him up to audition for Sebastian a few days later. Later that week, we presented Rogelio to Thomas Schumacher, who immediately signed off on this casting decision. Rogelio crossed Forty-Sixth Street from a swing contract at the Richard Rodgers Theatre to a principal role at the Lunt-Fontanne Theatre and played the role of Sebastian until *The Little*

---

* In musical theater, the term *swing* is often used to refer to a member of the company who understudies several chorus and/or dancing roles. If an understudy fills in for a lead role, a swing will act the parts normally performed by the understudy.

Mermaid closed in August 2009. Every time Rogelio did a talk-back with audiences following a performance, he mentioned timing—how you never know who's in the audience, and that he got discovered one rainy day by Jen Rudin at Disney because the star of the show was home suffering from Montezuma's revenge.

What's one of the biggest mistakes you've made at a Broadway audition?

Sometimes taking a big risk in an audition works, and sometimes it doesn't. When I first auditioned for *Hair* on Broadway, I decided to steadily undress as I performed, thinking that this would show the producers that I was comfortable with my body and free, since I felt that was what the show was about. I sang "Donna" from the show and rocked it. When I finished and looked at the silent and blank faces of the people behind the table, I knew they had not seen my vision. Finally, after what felt like an hour, the director very flatly asked if I would put my clothes back on.

—MANLEY POPE

— DOS AND DON'TS FOR — MUSICAL THEATER AUDITIONS

👍 DO be prepared on all the material (songs and scenes). Go through the acting scenes and figure out what your character wants and needs in the scene. Then figure out the conflict in the scene.

🖕 DO spend money on a ticket to see a show if it's currently playing on Broadway and you're auditioning to join the cast. You would be shocked at how many people came to audition for *Mary Poppins* having only seen the movie. If you can't see the show, there are many resources online now where performers can get a feel for a show or even see clips or hear the soundtracks for free. Do a search on www.spotify.com and www.youtube.com and see what's posted if you can't get to see the show live.

🖕 DO work with a vocal coach to learn the vocal material *correctly*. My top recommendation: www.bobmarks.com, or get referrals from friends.

🖕 DO organize sheet music in your music binder. Dividers can help. Make different sections for your various songs: up-tempo, ballad, contemporary pop-rock. A good vocal coach can help you organize your binder properly.

🖕 DO bring dance clothing if they ask you to. You may be asked to stay and dance if they like your singing voice.

🖕 DO be realistic about your talents. If the role calls for a five-foot-nine tenor who taps, make sure you're actually five foot nine and a tenor and can *really* tap. I've sat through many dance auditions over the years and watched many dancers fake their way through tap routines. Not fun for the dancers or for the creative team.

🖕 DO know your type. Are you an ingenue, leading man, character actress?

🖕 DO remember that a dance call is not a dance class. You need to show us you can learn choreography on the spot.

🖕 DO keep going to open calls.

🖕 DO keep up your vocal training.

- 👍 DO take a musical theater audition class or workshop, so that you get comfortable practicing how to audition in front of people. You can't be rusty when you go in for the real audition.

- 👎 DON'T sing a song that's out of your vocal range.

- 👎 DON'T use an audition to try out a song you've never sung before.

- 👎 DON'T call yourself "an actor who moves." Hone your dance skills. Grab a friend and take a dance class together. It's more productive (and fun) then spending an hour on the treadmill at the gym watching CNN. So many actors say they're a "good mover." That's not good enough.

JEN'S LAST WORD

99 Remember those famous lyrics from the song "What I Did for Love" from *A Chorus Line*? "Won't forget, can't regret what I did for love"? I sang that song for my first audition at Stagedoor Manor in 1982 when I was nine years old—completely inappropriate in subject matter and also completely out of my vocal range. Regardless, if you

love performing onstage and dream of Broadway, go for it. Train consistently with classes so you are ready to show your talents when you get to the Broadway audition. Then, when you get the role, make sure you can handle eight shows a week and the toll it can take on your voice and body. The audience has paid a lot of money to see you. Remember that every time you step out onto the stage, feel the lights of Broadway, and open your mouth to sing your show-stopping number!

CHAPTER SIX

GOING VIRAL

REALITY TV, WEBISODES, AND BECOMING A YOUTUBE SENSATION

When I was a child growing up in the 1980s, a person could become famous overnight by starring on a hit TV series or winning a popular television game show. But today, thanks to reality competition shows and videos gone viral, there are many more opportunities for instant celebrity. Anyone can become famous overnight. Just look at Honey Boo Boo. In most cases, instant stardom is less about talent than about personality.

The Reality of Reality Shows

Michael Warwick, the director of casting and talent development for A. Smith & Co. in Los Angeles, has been involved in reality projects since 1994. Warwick's first job in this medium was on an MTV special, *Real World Vacations*, based on MTV's hit franchise *The Real World*. He continued in the evolving field, first as a researcher on a hidden-camera show for MTV and then working his way up the ranks to being a producer on many projects for various British and American production companies. "In those days, there was no casting director," says Warwick. "Field producers or researchers just found the subjects for the projects on their own through phone calls, faxing, and handing out flyers."

Fast-forward to the year 2000, when *Survivor* debuted, modeled after the Swedish television series *Expedition Robinson*. In 2002 came *American Idol*, based on the popular British show *Pop Idol*. *American Idol* introduced the world to now-famous household names such as Carrie Underwood, Kelly Clarkson, Jennifer Hudson, Katharine McPhee, Jordin Sparks, and Clay Aiken. And the dueling, dynamic, dramatic personalities of Simon Cowell and Paula Abdul hooked viewers in to watch the show week after week.

Warwick sums up the differences between the early 1990s and today: "Back then the British called it 'factual entertainment,' since the projects weren't scripted, and in those days, the stories were more important. Today, it's the characters that are more important. You have to find people who are bigger than what they do. Look at Abby Lee Miller on *Dance Moms*. She could be a kindergarten teacher and we'd still watch. You could be the best blacksmith in the world, but if you don't have a personality that supersedes your profession, nobody cares and nobody will watch. There has to be conflict in every reality show. Everybody wants more drama."

How to Find Out About Casting for Reality Shows

In the 1990s, and up until just a few years ago, applicants for reality television went through a process that involved answering questions in a self-taped interview that they could record on a home camcorder. The interview was then mailed or FedExed to the reality show offices. Today, Skype is widely used for reality interviews. And Warwick confirms that if someone's personality is strong enough and shows through, they may actually get cast on the basis of a Skype session.

You can find out about reality casting by visiting www.realitywanted .com (or one of the other sites listed on pages 100–101) or through Facebook, Twitter, and Craigslist. All you need is a phone with access to social media to find out about reality postings. You have the potential to become famous by simply checking information on your phone. Scary or exciting? You be the judge!

Grease: You're the One That I Want!

NBC's reality show *Grease: You're the One That I Want!* aired in 2007. At first, I had no interest in watching. But because I loved the original movie *Grease* so much (the movie shares an elevated status with *The Brady Bunch* in my opinion), I decided to check out the show. I ended up watching, found myself caring about the outcome, and actually voted!

Here's what the show's winners, Laura Osnes and Max Crumm, and contestant Kate Rockwell had to share about their experiences with reality.

Red Bulls and Long Lines

In 2006, Max Crumm was a twenty-one-year-old actor living in L.A. He was in the shower when his roommate saw a commercial for the *Grease* reality show. They were holding auditions the next day. Max's roommate encouraged him to go and audition, certain he had the talent to win. That night, Max couldn't sleep, and decided it was a sign. So he got up at 5 A.M. and drove to the audition. After two Red Bulls and standing in line for four hours, Max made it past three rounds of singing and finally got to sing for the show's director, Kathleen Marshall. Several rounds later, he was chosen as one of the seven actors who would compete on the show for the role of Danny Zuko.

Max kept his expectations low throughout most of the episodes. He was convinced he wasn't going to win and just hoped that the national exposure would help him land a better agent. A naturally quirky type, he was even confused when he actually won the competition, convinced it was supposed to be Austin Miller or one of the other more traditionally attractive male contestants. Opening as Danny Zuko on Broadway later on in 2007 was bittersweet—both a dream come true and a rude awakening to the demands of Broadway.

Looking back, Max is thankful for the show. He never thought he'd get to do Broadway and he'll never take the experience on the reality show for granted. Today people still stop him on the street to tell him they voted for him. He thanks them and tells them they are the reason he gets to do what he loves. Max still watches reality shows, but has mild panic attacks when people start to get eliminated. "They are singing or cooking for their lives. Reality shows are my generation's way of getting ahead. If you have a good heart and are in the right place and working as hard as you can on a reality show, people will receive you and you will have a chance to do what it is you want to do."

ASK THE CASTING DIRECTOR

Does being a real actor hurt or help your chances of getting cast on reality shows?

I couldn't sell one show because the guy on the show (a former actor) was too nice. He wanted to use his acting skills to get on television. But he was too affable and didn't yell at people, so no one wanted to buy the show. Viewers want to see real people they can relate to on shows they love to watch and root for.

—MICHAEL WARWICK,
*director of casting and talent
development for A. Smith & Co.,
Los Angeles*

How *Grease: You're the One That I Want!* Brought a New Audience to Broadway

Today, Laura Osnes is a true Broadway star. She's originated and performed coveted roles on Broadway, including Nellie Forbush in the 2008 Broadway revival of *South Pacific*, Bonnie in *Bonnie & Clyde*, and, most recently, the title role in Broadway's *Cinderella*. But back in 2007, when she arrived to the open call for the *Grease* reality show, she was just one of a thousand standing in line, dreaming of Broadway.

"Nothing like this had ever been done in America. For me, the show was great exposure and opened up many doors. Today many people still wait for me at the stage door and say, 'I voted for you on *Grease!*'"

Upon reflection, the best part of the reality show in her estimation was that it brought a whole new audience to see *Grease* on Broadway. "I loved that so many families chose to make plans to visit New York to see a Broadway show instead of opting for a vacation at Disneyland. The reality show brought a new audience to Broadway."

The Dark Realities of Reality

When Kate Rockwell was chosen to compete on the *Grease* reality show, she recalls being told countless times by the network executives: "Your life is going to change. You're going to be TV stars and Broadway stars."

Years after the fact, Rockwell shared some of the negative parts of the experience: There was the brutal elimination process where the contestants stood in rows and sang "Tears on My Pillow" over and over for two hours. There were the day-to-day realities of the contestants being sequestered in a house, cut off from any Internet or cell phone reception and being transported to and from the rehearsals and tapings in a fifteen-passenger van. "We were supposed to be taken to the grocery store once a week, but often that wasn't the case. We couldn't make any plans because at any moment they might need one of us for an interview or rehearsal. There was a lot of manipulation and being left in the dark." Another tricky issue for Kate was the endless sound bites and interviews the contestants were asked to give. "When they needed a sound bite, you were not released until you said what they wanted you to say. Many times they wanted me to say, 'I should win this competition because I am the best singer here.'"

Despite these obstacles, Kate Rockwell has gone on to star on Broadway in numerous productions, including *Hair*, *Legally Blonde*, *Bring It On: The Musical*, and *Rock of Ages*, in which she played the lead role, Sherrie.

Ali Stroker's experience as a contestant on *The Glee Project* mirrored many of the stories that Kate shared with me. Ali got involved when she saw a casting call posted on Facebook. She posted her video submissions on Myspace and on *The Glee Project*'s own website. Ali quickly discovered through the casting process that in reality shows, it's not just about choosing the most talented people but choosing the best pieces to fit the overall puzzle.

Once she was on the show, Ali's life changed completely. Thousands of people were following her on social media and rooting for her on a show where she played herself. This was a new world for Ali, who came from theater. "After a show, people wait to meet you outside the stage door. There's so much more exposure when you're on national TV."

And there were the rules of reality on *The Glee Project*. Everyone's privacy was invaded. The group lived together in one room with no full walls. Participants were not allowed to leave the house or to speak at meals. Ali sums it up: "With no phone or computer distractions or contact with other people, you are forced to focus on what you are doing, which is competing, and this helps to raise the stakes. The further away you are from actual reality, the more important the competition feels and seems, and that's one way the shows get their drama."

In the end, Ali was grateful for the opportunity. She ended up doing a guest spot on *Glee*. "It's totally my world. A little pop. A little underdog."

Helpful Websites for Reality Audition Information

www.realitywanted.com

www.sirlinksalot.net/castingcalls.html

www.starnow.com

www.mtv.com/ontv/castingcall

www.castingcallhub.com/tryout/reality-tv

www.nonscripted.tv

www.craigslist.org (look under creative gigs)

www.twitter.com (use the search function or hashtags)

And be sure to check out Facebook for reality casting notes and announcements. There are many casting and audition groups like Put Me on TV. You don't even have to have a computer. A good smartphone that's connected to social media can provide all the information you need to find out about the latest reality casting opportunities.

Tips for a Great Reality Show Audition

- **Be yourself.** If you're trying out for a *Survivor*-type show, make sure you genuinely want to have an outdoor experience. If you're auditioning for a vocal talent competition, you'd better like to sing. If you try being someone you're not, it will show, and you likely will not make it past the first round of auditions.

- **Be selective.** If you keep submitting for every single reality show and you're not selective, the casting directors and field producers will start recognizing you and possibly ignore your audition tapes. It's the equivalent of an actor submitting for every role, even when they don't fit the age, gender, or ethnicity in the casting breakdown. This drives us casting directors crazy! The market is saturated with applicants; please don't be the guy who applies to every single show.

- **Personality is key!** If you have a great personality, it will shine through no matter what the medium: phone interview, video, even a Skype interview.

AUDITION
STORIES

EPIC SUCCESS

I had an epic success at an audition for FOX's *Glee*. We were told to prepare a song to sing that would showcase an impressive belter range. They gave examples like Lady Gaga's "Edge of Glory" and Kelly Clarkson's "Stronger." They were looking for powerful showstoppers. With a few days to prepare, I went with the more classic choice of "Ain't No Mountain High Enough." The waiting room for the audition was intimidating, filled with over-eighteen-year-olds and Broadway veterans galore. But with my acoustic guitar by my side (just in case I was asked to sing a different song with a different vibe), my pink dress, and my own personality, I realized I was unique and I would do the best I could. Once I was called into the audition room, I was asked to sing my song. I belted away, more than pleased with my performance. Once I finished, the casting director said, "That was good! Now I want it transposed a full step up and for you to sing it in that key now. You can do that, right? I just want to know that you can reach those notes." I was already belting Cs and Ds, and any singer knows how terrifying transposing on the spot can be. However, I confidently nodded my head and sang every note perfectly, staying focused. Once I was done, the casting director immediately told me she loved me and wanted me to come in for a callback. Confidence and determination will always go a long way!

—HEATHER BRAVERMAN,
age sixteen

How to Become a YouTube Sensation

If you opt not to pursue a reality show, there's always YouTube. Dani Shay hails from Orlando, Florida, and has been a singer-songwriter for the past seven years. Three years ago, when Justin Bieber hit the scene, people started to tell her that she looked like him. One Thanksgiving, she was working at her parents' shoe store at the local shopping mall in Orlando and was mobbed on a lunch break by crazed Bieber fans.

Later that day, Dani looked him up and was shocked to see how much he really did look like her. She promptly wrote a parody of his hit song "Baby" called "What the Hell" and released a video of it in December 2010. She also made a video and cover of Eminem's "Love the Way You Lie." Both videos went viral in early 2011 and she became an immediate YouTube sensation. Pop tastemakers posted the videos and they spread like wildfire. Perez Hilton, Yahoo!, World Star Hip Hop, and *OK!* magazine posted the videos. No surprise: Dani's YouTube inbox filled up with offers.

America's Got Talent reached out to Dani to see if she'd audition for the show. At first she resisted and wondered if doing a reality show would make her an immediate sellout or less of an artist. Then she remembered her goal: to reach people with her music. She flew to Houston to audition. After appearing on *America's Got Talent*, she next appeared on *The Glee Project*.

I asked Dani how her career has changed after the YouTube videos and reality shows. Her music has gone global, with 117,000 Facebook fans and 64,000 Twitter followers experiencing her music videos in places as far-flung as Malaysia, Australia, and Africa. She credits Twitter for allowing her to make incredible connections through just a simple 140-character message.

Going Viral: The Best Sites to Post Your Videos

There are countless sites where users can post videos that have the potential to go viral. Here are my top three, in order of preference:

1. **YouTube:** Easy to use and a destination for casting directors and producers to view your material. Raymond J. Lee has had numerous videos that have gone viral thanks to YouTube. "I think if you put out a good video that's funny or fun, that's the best way to attempt a viral video. YouTube is an amazing platform to get your material seen. Because of my own videos that have gone viral, I've been able to get work and people know what I can do as a filmmaker."

2. **Vimeo:** Many agents and managers use this to pitch their clients' reels. It's usually password protected and the video quality is very clear. Vimeo is professional and easy to use.

3. **Twitter:** Posting your videos here works for
   social stuff, but I think it's better to use a more
   professional site like YouTube or Vimeo first,
   then people can tweet your videos from there.

Webisodes and the Evolution of the Web Series

Many actors act in or create webisodes as a creative outlet and to increase acting opportunities. A webisode is an episode of a series available online either for download or for instant streaming. Webisodes are distributed through video-sharing sites such as Vimeo or YouTube. While there is no set standard for length, most webisodes are relatively short, ranging from three to fifteen minutes in length.

Creating Her Own Work:
Julia Tokarz and *It's Not Okay, Cupid!*

Actress Julia Tokarz writes, produces, directs, and stars in a Web series called *It's Not Okay, Cupid!* with Stefanie Grassley, a fellow alumna from the Upright Citizen's Brigade (UCB) theater.[*] Before this series, she acted in a few webisodes written, produced, and directed by UCB alumni who posted auditions on the UCB website. Julia shared the basic details:

> Most webisodes are nonunion and are for gaining exposure. There's usually no pay. You show up and there's free food. The time commitment is normally one to two days.
>
> I think that for people who are interested in comedy and improv it's a great medium for us to showcase our work and get it out there. For people outside of the box who don't book shows, it's nice to be

---

[*] UCB has branches in New York and L.A. and offers improve comedy, sketch-writing, and storytelling classes, among others. Check out www.ucbtheatre.com.

able to write and have our work shown, especially if you like to write. Webisodes are so easy because you can include a link in an e-mail and people can just click on it and share it. We are still developing and creating it to what fits us better, but in terms of creativity, it is definitely the most creative venture I've undertaken and it's very fulfilling. It's really hard not having money to back you up and no real support. It takes a certain personality in order to do all this. But it's so worth it. It's really rewarding watching people watch your work. We just won five awards at the L.A. Web Festival.

Visit www.itsnotokaycupidtheseries.com for more details.

ASK THE ACTOR ★

What's the payoff for actors who do webisodes?

When you're an artist you like to be part of something creative. So when friends are doing things that they believe in, it's sexy. It's sexy when people are passionate about something. To see someone excited about making a webisode is infectious and you want to be part of it too! Also, as an actor you can put your work from a webisode into a reel and show people later what you did.

—MIKE KELTON,
www.mikekelton.com

No Other Hands in the Creative Kitchen: It Could Be Worse

Actors Wesley Taylor and Mitchell Jarvis met back in 2008 in the original off-Broadway cast of *Rock of Ages*. As part of the show's marketing campaign, actors in the cast were given flip cameras and asked to start filming themselves going out to eat, or on their lunch break. The footage would be used on the show's website.

Wesley and Mitchell put up twelve minutes of raw footage, but found it boring and unfocused. They joined with their cast mate Lauren Molina and decided to make "mockumentary" sketches backstage. They started recording cast mates backstage in costume. The videos quickly went from mockumentary to genre parody.

Wesley left *Rock of Ages* to perform on Broadway in *The Addams Family*. Despite the new gig, he missed collaborating with Mitch and Lauren, so they started a sketch show called *Billy Green* that became wildly popular. As a result, Wesley and Mitchell gained a fan base as people started following them on their YouTube channel.

After fifteen hundred performances of *Rock of Ages* for Mitchell and four hundred for Wesley in *The Addams Family*, they joined forces to create the successful Web series *It Could Be Worse*. Initially, creating their own Web series was a way to keep flexing their creative muscles. "We're smart people creating work," Wesley observed. "This comes from a place where you feel creatively stifled because you're doing the same show over and over again. You feel like the industry is expecting only one thing from you. You know they always say New York is better than L.A. at not putting you in a box, but New York is also really bad at it."

Mitchell and Wesley are a two-person crew. Mitchell bought a camera (a Canon EOS Rebel T3i), spray-painted two umbrellas white, and bought six floodlights to use for lighting their sets. He plugs a microphone into the camera, which other technicians laugh at him for. They coedit on Final Cut X, codirect, and cowrite each episode. Wesley is in charge of casting, scheduling, and location scouting. They often pay to use space, or opt to use a lot of friends' apartments. They even managed to turn Mitchell's apartment into an Asian brothel for one episode. Visit www.itcouldbeworse.tv to watch some of the episodes yourself!

Getting Cast in a Webisode

Many webisodes are self-generated work and the creators often don't hire casting directors. If that's the case, here's how to get involved:

- Take an improv class. You'll meet other creative people like yourself. In addition to having fun and learning valuable acting skills, you will network and make friends who could turn into potential future collaborators.

- Connect with improv people through social media. They will likely post or tweet if they are looking for actors.

- Volunteer to help out at a friend's webisode shoot. You never know . . . you could end up getting a role!

What Makes a Webisode Popular?

Webisode viewers are loyal, just like regular television viewers. Your taste will dictate which webisodes you like to watch. When you like a series, tweet about it so more people will start to watch. Here's where social media can work in a positive way!

There are some fantastic Web series out there, and if you're interested in acting in your own, you should be familiar with the medium. For humor, I recommend checking out *Submissions Only, Comedians in Cars Getting Coffee* (Jerry Seinfeld's Web series), *Dora the Explorer and the Destiny Medallion* (starring Ariel Winter from *Modern Family*), and *In Bed with Joan*, starring Joan Rivers. For the hipster crowd, try *High Maintenance*.

The list goes on and on. The bottom line? Creative people are making interesting, new content and producing webisodes every day, and this trend will only continue. Fans stay loyal with webisodes that are honest, well written, and well shot. And since webisodes are short, it's a perfect break in the middle of a hectic day. Plus, you can enjoy watching on your various devices while on the go.

Hulu, Netflix, Yahoo!, and Amazon Original Programming

In addition to television shows, Hulu, Netflix, Yahoo!, and Amazon are launching into production with scripted shows of their own. More media-scripted programming provides even more opportunities for actors. Rachel Resheff, age thirteen, was cast in an episode of *Orange Is the New Black* for Netflix. Her audition experience was just like a network audition for any other scripted programming. The pay and the filming were equivalent to what she'd been paid in regular network situations. And the set was similar to that of any network show, with a professional crew. Although the distribution for this type of content is vastly different than for a network series, these are still professionally produced shows and their producers will expect the same high standards from actors cast in them.

JEN'S LAST WORD

" Yes, reality TV is here to stay. Proceed cautiously, and make sure you are ready for the realities of reality.

You too can be a YouTube sensation. But make sure you know what you want when you post a video. To gain more fans? To get discovered and experience potential fast fame? Make sure you are proud of your video before you upload it, because once it's posted, it's viral.

Webisodes are a great way to get experience in front of the camera. Just make sure that if you choose to donate your time and talents, the webisode is worth it and a positive experience. If you choose to make your own, be prepared to spend money (as much as $5,000 to $7,000 per episode) to make the finished product look great.

So go ahead. Go viral.

CHAPTER SEVEN

MAKING MICKEY TALK

VOICE-OVER AND ANIMATION AUDITIONS

'm ten years old and it's my first voice-over audition for South Carolina National Bank. My only speaking line is: "Daddy, am I a deduction?" and the father says, "Yes, my favorite one." The following afternoon, my manager calls and tells me they're choosing between me and one other girl. She puts me on hold* for the voice-over recording date. I lie awake all night praying to God to please choose me for the voice.

The next day I find out that I didn't get chosen for the South Carolina spot, but my managers are very impressed that I got so close. They assure me I'm a natural for voice-overs. The next year I book the voice of Beezus in a series of Ramona Quimby audiobooks.

Tips for Voice-Over Auditions

There's a perception that voice-over work is easy. Trust me, it's not. Voice acting is a craft that requires practice and unique skills. A few lines of commercial copy can look deceptively easy, but a lot more work goes into perfectly

---

* Also known as *first refusal*. When a producer likes you, you may be put *on hold*. This is a courtesy to let you know that you are being seriously considered for that project and tell you what dates to "hold" in case the producer decides to hire you.

voicing a line than meets the eye. Actors need to become familiar with voice-over booth logistics and how to use the microphone and headphones.

Here are a few basic tips:

- The microphone picks up all kinds of sounds when recording. You can hear everything: a dry mouth, a lisp, any speech issues. Make sure to drink lots of water before your audition.

- Nibble an apple. The juice from the apple helps to moisten your mouth so you won't sound dry.

- Arrive a few minutes early to look over the commercial copy. Most of the time you will not receive scripts in advance.

- During your audition, play with your vocal highs and lows.

- Tell the story of the script with your voice.

- Keep your reads conversational.

- Think about pacing and pitch.

Celebrity Casting for Voice-Over Campaigns

The voice-over market has drastically changed over the years since companies began hiring celebrities to voice major campaigns. Remember when Julia Roberts was the new voice for America Online? This was one of the early instances of celebrity voice-overs in advertising, and today there are fewer and fewer voice-over jobs left for noncelebrities. Listen closely the next time a car commercial airs on television. The male voice may be

Kevin Spacey (Honda), Tim Allen (Chevrolet), Jon Hamm (Mercedes-Benz), or Jeff Bridges (Hyundai)—to name just a few.

How has the voice-over business changed since you started as an agent twenty years ago?

When I started out, an agent could not represent enough forty-to-sixty-year-old male announcers with deep "voice of God" sounds. Now advertisers are looking mainly for actors with a more casual, conversational, real delivery, as if the actor is just talking to the person on the other side of the television or radio.

When I listen to actors' commercial voice samples, I am listening for range in their delivery and tone. The more an actor can vary his or her delivery, the more opportunities he or she will have to work. Show what you do best. Don't overload your audition recording with too many samples that may not be your best work simply to show range.

—JEB BERNSTEIN,
commercial voice-over agent,
Paradigm

Celebrity Casting in Animated Films

During my years at Disney Animation (2002 to 2007), the animation industry transitioned from traditional hand-drawn (2-D) animation to computer-generated (3-D) animation. This was a very hard time for many

Disney animators. In addition to the switch from 2-D to 3-D, every other major studio (and some independent studios) began producing animated films. The market was soon saturated with animated films all competing at the box office. Celebrity casting became the norm, and Disney tried to keep up.

Before the celebrity casting trend began, most of the roles were voiced by voice-over and theater actors. If you look at the cast lists for legendary animated movies like *The Lion King, Aladdin, Hercules,* and *Tarzan,* you'll see wonderful casts assembled with a few recognizable names from the theater world, but not many famous TV or film actors.

Animated feature celebrity casting began around 2000 and has continued ever since. In addition to casting celebrities, 3-D animated features were now faster, funnier, and more contemporary in music choices, bathroom humor, and overall tone.

During the early years of celebrity casting, Brad Pitt, Will Smith, Jack Black, Renée Zellweger, and Angelina Jolie began voicing roles for some of the DreamWorks animated movies. Getting celebrities on a talk-show couch to promote the movies provided a boost to the weekly box office numbers. A celebrity seemed a necessity to help the movie survive the box office every weekend. We tried to keep up at Disney, and I often found myself chasing celebrities at various Hollywood events and comedy festivals.

I have mixed opinions on celebrity casting. On the plus side, it's easier to schedule celebrities to do voice-over work than a live-action shoot, since we usually record just one actor at a time and don't have to coordinate multiple actors' availability. During my years at Disney, we could always find a four-hour session on a day off from their film shoot or their current TV series schedule. Interest from the celebrity, not availability, was a dictating factor. Over the years we recorded Billy Connolly from Malta, Steve Zahn from Africa, and the Duchess of York, Sarah Ferguson, from England, all through video conferencing. Many celebs love getting to show up at the recording studio in sweats without having to worry about hair and makeup.

Some celebrities are great at telling stories with their voices, while others lack texture and vocal highs and lows that make for an interesting voice. Many just aren't natural at this genre. They need hair, makeup, and the camera in order to tell a story. And since most agents won't let their famous clients audition, it's hard to know whether or not a particular actor will be comfortable behind the microphone.

— ASK THE —
ACTOR

Should a voice-over actor invest in a home studio?

Auditions and jobs can often come at the last minute. In today's fast-paced market, every working voice actor needs some sort of home studio. It can be very simple and the cost is not high. You need a decent microphone (there are many good ones in the $300 range), a mic stand, a pre-amp that the mic is plugged into and then plugged into your laptop, and a quiet closet or small room. Should cost $500 to $1,000 total for a very good booth. I used a company called Sweetwater to make my choices and turned my coat closet into my recording booth.

—JASON HARRIS,
*busy voice over actor; voice director;
and dubbing coordinator, owner,
and operator of
www.theloopingdivision.com*

— ASK THE —
DIRECTOR

What do you listen for when directing voice actors?

The director is listening for a performance that comes completely through the voice. If the director isn't watching your performance, no worries. They want to hear what the actor is saying and not be swayed by what the actor is doing. On *Toy Story 2*, I remember having to force myself to not watch Tom Hanks while directing him from the booth—many times he would do something that was visually hilarious, but it wasn't always there on the sound track.

—ASH BRANNON,
director, Surf's Up, *and codirector*,
Toy Story 2

The Princess and the Frog:
Casting Disney's First African American Princess

I'm very proud of the animated feature films I cast during my five years as director of casting at Walt Disney Animation Studios in Burbank, California. The talking animal movies include *Brother Bear* (2003), *Chicken Little* (2005), and *The Wild* (2006). Talking superheroes, robots, and royalty include *The Incredibles* (2004), *Meet the Robinsons* (2006), *The Princess and the Frog* (2009), and *Frankenweenie* (2012).

The Princess and the Frog brought Disney back to traditional hand-drawn 2-D animation and the animated musical—what Disney does best. The most crucial role to cast was Princess Tiana, Disney's first African American princess. In 2004, Anika Noni Rose won a Tony Award* for her performance in the critically acclaimed Broadway show *Caroline, or Change*. Later that year, Anika reprised her role at the Ahmanson Theatre in Los Angeles.

_____

* The Antoinette Perry Award for Excellence in Theatre, more commonly known informally as the Tony Award, recognizes achievement in live Broadway theater. The awards are presented by the American Theatre Wing and the Broadway League at an annual ceremony in New York City. The awards are given for Broadway productions and performances, with one award given for regional theatre. The awards are named after Antoinette Perry, cofounder of the American Theatre Wing.

During that trip, Anika came by the animation studio to meet with me. At the time there was one beautiful drawing of an African American princess upstairs on the development floor. After she signed my *Caroline, or Change* CD, I casually mentioned that if we ever had a role for an African American princess, she'd be perfect. (Years later, when the movie came out, Anika mentioned this conversation in an interview for *People* magazine.)

Fast-forward to November 2006: Legendary animation directors Ron Clements and John Musker (*Hercules, Aladdin, The Little Mermaid, Pocahontas*) developed a full script for *The Princess and the Frog,* set in New Orleans in the 1920s. Randy Newman came on board as the composer. Disney green-lit* the movie. My phone started to ring off the hook.

Beyoncé, Tyra Banks, and Alicia Keys all wanted to play this coveted role. I started to set up auditions in Los Angeles, New York, and New Orleans. Anika was the very first actress that I brought in to audition for Ron, John, and producer Peter Del Vecho. Anika sang three contrasting songs that showed her incredible vocal range and competitive notes (the high notes!) and then performed the audition scenes. We all agreed that her voice sounded completely believable as a girl living in New Orleans in the 1920s. I knew deep down that Anika was perfect for this role.

We continued to audition actresses in New York, Los Angeles, and New Orleans. A month after Anika's initial audition, the movie version of *Dreamgirls* opened, starring Anika, Beyoncé, and a former American Idol contestant named Jennifer Hudson. Beyoncé's agent kept calling me to campaign for the *Princess and the Frog* role, but insisted she was "offer only," which meant we would have to offer her the role without her coming in to audition. *Dreamgirls* was a big hit, and newcomer Jennifer Hudson walked off with all the awards. We went through the process of scheduling Jennifer's audition, which took several months, since she was busy recording a new album. Alicia Keys auditioned three times and even worked with

---

* To *green-light* is to give permission or a go ahead to move forward with a project.

a dialect coach to perfect a New Orleans accent. Throughout all this, Anika waited patiently as we worked through our casting process.

AUDITION STORIES

EPIC FAIL

On my very first audition I got a horrible bloody nose on the way, but I was a four-year-old little trouper and ended up getting on hold for the commercial. But my second audition was a huge fail. My agents had told my dad to tell me to say I was five, so when they asked me how old I was I said: "Well, I'm four years old, but my daddy told me to say that I'm five." Out the door!

—KIRRILEE BERGER,
age thirteen

Making the Final Casting Decision for Princess Tiana

We were five months into our casting process. My close friend and colleague Tim Curtis, now a partner at WME Entertainment, was the agent who represented Anika Noni Rose, Alicia Keys, and Jennifer Hudson. We'd talk every day during these final weeks of the casting process, trying to predict which actress would win the coveted role. Alicia had an overall talent deal with Disney, so casting her would have made sense politically. But while her smoky sound and vocal texture were amazing, I just didn't believe her voice belonged to a princess who lived in New Orleans in the 1920s. Jennifer was the "it" girl at the time, but I still believed that Anika was the best actress to voice the role. Tim mused, "When this casting process is over, I'm going to have one thrilled client and two heartbroken ones."

At the final hour, Jennifer fell out of the casting mix and a New York actress named Montego Glover took a top spot. Our editors took audition voice samples from Anika, Alicia, and Montego and cut the auditions

Anika Noni Rose looked stunning on the red carpet for The Princess and the Frog's *premiere in 2009.*

against images of Princess Tiana. John, Ron, Peter, and I sat in a casting meeting with our executives. We closed our eyes and listened to the three voices. Before coming to a consensus, we asked the age-old question: "Is this the right voice to come out of the character?" This was to be a historic casting decision, not only because it was a major movie in the very competitive arena of animation, but also because we were choosing the voice for Disney's first African American princess. In the end, we chose Anika!

Here's why I love this casting story:

- We actually got to cast our top choice for the role.
- I'd predicted this when Anika and I met back at Disney in 2004.
- The movie opened well and brought some much needed success to Disney's animation division.

Me with Anika Noni Rose at the L.A. premiere of The Princess and the Frog, *2009.*
(ARDEN RODGERS)

— ASK THE —
ACTOR
★

What was it like to voice the role of Dash in **The Incredibles?**

For most ten-year-olds, the concept of excitement is usually surrounded by things like staying up past nine on a school night or watching an episode of *South Park* while their parents are asleep. So for me, landing a lead role in a Pixar film at such a young age far surpassed excitement and delved into a realm that can only be described as frantic euphoria. It was thrilling, it was scary, it was hectic, and it was probably my first taste of accomplishment. Although I didn't quite have the brainpower or maturity to come to terms with how big a deal it was, I just felt this immense pride for what I had gotten myself into. The experience itself, missing a week of school to spend two insane days at Pixar

Studios working with the insanely genius ball of human energy that is Brad Bird, and to see firsthand the process of creating an animated film, was more than I could have ever imagined.

—SPENCER FOX,
age eighteen

_ VOICE-OVER AND ANIMATION _ AUDITION DOS AND DON'TS

If you want to pursue the voice-over/animation area, here are some important tips to remember:

- DO take a voice-over/animation class or workshop. Seasoned animation actors like Bob Bergen and Pat Fraley teach workshops in Los Angeles and New York. Visit www.bobbergen.com and www.patfraley.com to see when their next workshops are. Spend time in the recording studio practicing and learning from these guys.

- DO keep your reads well paced and in your regular voice, unless the role asks for big, cartoony voices and characters.

- DO think real. Voice-over has evolved, just like commercials. Throw lines away. Be casual and conversational instead of announcer-y and formal.

- DO talk with a smile.

- DO use your vocal highs and lows. We use different vocal tones of our voice every day. Listen to what you sound like when you're asking for something, talking to your mother, or talking to a five-year-old child.

- DO spend money on a good demo. Ideally your demo should have different sections—animation, promo, and commercials. The quality needs to be professional.

- DO consider building a home studio.

- DO know your medium: watch a lot of animation and understand the differences in tone. Tom Kenny's vocal pacing is fast and energetic when he's voicing Spongebob. On the opposite end of the spectrum, Craig T. Nelson's Mr. Incredible voice sounds like a real person who just happens to be animated.

- DO send your demo out to voice-over agents, once you make a good one.

- DON'T try to make a demo on your iPhone.

JEN'S LAST WORD

" Just because you're talented in one area doesn't automatically qualify you as an expert in all areas. Be honest with yourself about your strengths. Take classes and workshops to improve your skills. Voice acting is largely about pacing, vocal texture, and quality. Sometimes an actor needs hair and makeup and the camera to tell their story; their voice is just not enough. Actors may want to be skilled in all areas, but no one is superhuman. Except maybe Dash in *The Incredibles.*

CHAPTER EIGHT

CAN YOU HEAR ME NOW?

COMMERCIAL AUDITIONS

'm eleven years old and at the final audition for a bologna commercial. My mother has insisted I wear my sister's bright pink OshKosh jumper, which I hate. When the director instructs me to eat the premade bologna sandwich on the prop table, I make a face and tell him I hate bologna. The next day I find out I've booked the commercial.

The next week, my mother and I arrive at the commercial shoot. I gasp when I spot a prop table with about fifty premade bologna sandwiches on thick white Wonder bread. "I can't eat them," I whisper to my mother conspiratorially. Her response: "Eat the bologna, Jennifer, and think about the residuals." *

She was right. The bologna commercial aired for close to ten years. The residuals paid for braces, a Macintosh laptop when I graduated college, and some travel abroad. I'll never know why I booked the commercial—was it my glasses, my scowl, or that horrid pink OshKosh jumper? Thirty years later I still can't look at a bologna sandwich on white bread without feeling nauseated.

---

* *Residuals* are payments made to union actors when their performance is used multiple times. There are different pay scales for different types of work (TV, film, commercials), which are dictated by different contracts (low budget, made for cable, feature films, national network usage, etc.).

Can You Hear Me Now?
The Post-9/11 Search for the Verizon Guy

Right after September 11, 2001, I was a casting associate at Susan Shop-maker Casting, and we were hired to cast a campaign for a new phone company called Verizon. We were tasked to find a spokesman distinctly different from Carrot Top on the 1-800 Call ATT spots and the business-man in the suit on the Sprint commercials. I auditioned hundreds of men of all ethnicities and ages for weeks on end, all saying that now-famous line: "Can you hear me now?" The actors would crawl around the audition studio talking on the Verizon phone, pretending to be in different locations such as a tunnel, the desert, or a mountaintop in Nepal.

On one of the final casting days, Paul Marcarelli walked into the room. I just knew he'd book the spot before he even slated* his name. Paul was engaging and hip and wore cool black glasses. He got the commercial. The campaign went global and the commercials are still on the air. Lesson: Go to any and every commercial audition. You never know when you'll be the perfect fit.

AGENT'S CORNER

What's your best advice for actors who want to work in commercials?

Treat commercials like a job. Be professional by confirming appointments, showing up on time, dressing appropriately, and being prepared. The commercial world moves too quickly to accommodate "artistic temperaments." Also, communicate with your agents: always discuss issues of availability and ask any questions

---

* An actor's *slate* is a spoken on-camera introduction with the actor's name, age (if under eighteen years old), height, and sometimes agency or hometown. The actor talks to the camera and introduces him- or herself with these important details.

about potential conflicts. This will head off any potential problems before they cause difficulties for casting directors and producers and, consequently, agents and talent. Finally, the most successful actors in commercials enjoy the process—they like getting to play different roles, to meet the various people involved in the business, and get dressed up and act in front of the camera. They approach it like a business but also a little like play. They are interested and happy to be in the room. This spirit definitely communicates itself and makes everyone want to work with you either now . . . or in the future.

—TRACEY GOLDBLUM,
Abrams Artists Agency

Logistics of Commercial Auditions

Commercials auditions are fast and furious, with a potentially lucrative outcome. Casting sessions are often very last minute. It's not uncommon to get a call in the morning for an audition later that day. When your agent calls you with the audition information, they'll often tell you the role you're auditioning for, such as young mom, office worker, doctor, tech geek, hipster, or waitress.

In the 1980s the actors featured in commercials really sold products with big voices and dramatic flair. Today commercials tend toward a more "realistic" feel, both cinematically and from an acting perspective. Less is more. The humor comes from the situation, rather than from actors punching up the comedy.

The commercial business has also changed financially and creatively over the years. To save money, many advertising agencies now hire nonunion actors and offer a buyout fee for the shoot (paying one lump sum up front instead of residual payments over time). There are fewer national network spots. Today commercials are often unscripted. In these cases, actors are given a scenario, then expected to improvise in the audition room.

Next time you're watching television, instead of fast-forwarding through the commercials, watch a few spots. Describe the acting style and overall tone of the commercial. This will help you prepare when you start to audition.

— ASK THE —
ACTOR
★

Are improv classes helpful for commercial auditions?

Improv classes teach you to be present, to listen, to think quickly on your feet, to be able to speak as a character, and to work well with a partner. Don't try to be funny. Play the character sincerely and the humor will come. Upright Citizens Brigade (UCB) teaches actors to play at the top of their intelligence. Never pander or play "down." Your audience is smarter than you think.

—REBECKA RAY

The Commercial Callback

If you're lucky enough to get called back for the commercial, the callback will take place with the director, producer, and various people from the advertising agency. Actors are assigned specific appointment times at the callback, and are often mixed and matched and brought in in groups. You may be asked to do more improv or get paired up with different actors if the commercial calls for a family or a group of office workers. Be patient. Prepare to stay. Many times the creative team needs to look at groups of actors together to assemble and ultimately populate the perfect cast.

There are many creative and business people involved in casting commercials. Final casting choices are made by the director, producers, and advertising agency executives. The top talent choices are presented to the client (the people who work at Charmin or Hasbro or whatever company is selling the product), who weigh in with their final approval. When you have millions of dollars at stake with every commercial, it can create an obvious pressure cooker.

Don't get freaked out if twelve people are in the room eating sushi or texting and appear uninterested. They are. And even if you don't book the commercial, you should still feel good about getting a callback. Someone on the creative team liked you, and that's a good thing. In the end, you may go on dozens of commercial auditions before you get cast, but keep trying and take every audition as an opportunity to be seen.

AUDITION STORIES

EPIC SUCCESS

A friend called me after her audition for a Playtex Bra commercial. She said, "Rena, you have to get an appointment for this commercial! They're looking for funny girls with big boobs who can do improv!" I called my commercial agent, who informed me that I wasn't the right type. They were looking for larger women, and she couldn't get me an appointment. I asked if I should crash the audition. She said, "We don't recommend that, but if you feel strongly about it then just know we didn't tell you to do it." Well . . . I felt strongly about it. I walked to the casting office. The casting director was finishing her lunch. I said "Hi. I'm a 34DD and would love to audition." She told me to go in the back and put on a Playtex bra. They put me on tape. I ended up booking the Playtex 18 Hour bra campaign, which ran for two and a half years, paid my rent, and got me three years of union health insurance.

—RENA STROBER,
www.RenaStrober.com

AGENT'S CORNER

How has the commercial business changed over your many years as an agent?

The biggest change in the past twenty years has been in the proliferation of nonunion commercial work. The Internet has prompted huge changes in the commercial business. As a platform for viewing commercials, it allows advertisers to target their market much more specifically and at a much lower cost. As a tool for the casting process, it allows more actors from a greater geographical area to be considered for the same role, as more commercials are regularly being cast in multiple cities. Coupled with the commercial business's demand for new types, this has generated more commercial actors in the business, creating greater competition for the better jobs.

—MICKEY SHERA,
*Innovative Artists Talent
and Literary Agency*

COMMERCIAL AUDITION
DOS AND DON'TS

👎 DON'T experiment with new clothing, especially on the day of the audition.

👎 DON'T wear turtlenecks, stripes, or crazy patterns. They can be distracting to the viewers watching your audition.

👍 DO dress in solid colors.

👍 DO purchase a white "uniform" shirt, for when you're the waiter, server, cashier, nurse, doctor. A white blouse or dress shirt will suffice. And conversely, a dark shirt works best for a cop.

👍 DO buy a nice suit to play an upscale businessperson, lawyer, or detective. Nice also means well pressed. Splurge on dry-cleaning when you can. Or buy a steam iron at any drugstore.

👍 DO write down what outfit you wear to each commercial audition. Then plan to wear the same outfit to the callback.

ASK THE
ACTOR
⭐

What's the craziest wardrobe request you've had for a commercial audition?

For theater, film, and (most) TV, they don't expect you to come into the audition dressed in costume for the character. Just something respectful, maybe the suggestion of a costume. But for commercials, it helps to show you're the character through wardrobe.

I remember getting a call once from my commercial agent. She said: "You have an audition tomorrow to play a clown. Wear something bright and colorful. If you own a clown suit, please wear it." I didn't own a clown suit. And I didn't get the part, either.

—JASON KRAVITS,
www.jasonkravits.net

STAGE MOMS' CORNER

Kids should arrive to the commercial audition in regular clothing, unless your agent says otherwise. Converse sneakers, jeans, and a solid shirt are perfect for most commercial auditions. Many times kids will be matched up with actors playing other family members. Looks, likability, and personality are key factors that determine which kids get cast.

JEN'S LAST WORD

" The world of commercials is more fast-paced than other types of auditions. Here are a few final tips to remember when auditioning for commercials:

- Have fun. Seriously, if you can't have fun at a silly commercial audition, get a job crunching numbers at a desk.

- Be flexible.

- Think on your feet.

- Once the audition is over, try to forget about it and get on with your day. Who knows, maybe you could book a bologna commercial or a new campaign for Verizon when you least expect it.

CHAPTER NINE

DON'T TWEET US, WE'LL TWEET YOU

USING TECHNOLOGY TO HELP YOUR CAREER

I n 1982 my family bought our first answering machine. The machine came with a device to check the messages, and we loved calling in to hear the new messages. My heart always skipped a beat when my manager would leave details on the machine for an upcoming audition. In 1985, we celebrated my TV movie airing by purchasing a new VCR to replace the old VHS machine my grandma Betty had loaned us. In 1988, my sister left for college with an IBM computer, and in 1989, I used my first Macintosh SE computer. The technology story goes on and on!

Here we are today, trapped in the digital age and a world of instant celebrity stardom. We're addicted to Facebook, Twitter, Instagram, Tumblr, YouTube, and Vine. Our hands are busy all day texting, blogging, and e-mailing from our various devices. Our attention spans are shorter. We're constantly consumed by new sites, new apps, new phones, and new gadgets. We can't imagine any other world. Information attacks us from thousands of websites and blogs that provide information about auditions. As a result, actors often find themselves drowning in an oversaturation of what can frequently be the wrong information.

In some ways, technology has made our lives easier. We have PDF versions of scripts and JPGs of head shots. And much of the casting process takes place online: breakdowns are released electronically, submissions are viewed online. Demo reels and voice-over demos are all digital. Actors can send in self-tapes for projects that are casting. Our technological world is moving faster and faster. Our brains must keep up or we'll miss out.

Technology can help your acting career, but only if you navigate it carefully.

Making a Website

The first step for any actor is to create a basic website that includes a contact link, photos, a résumé, demo reels (if you have them), and reviews or other press clips. Check out your actor friends' websites, or those of the many actors interviewed throughout this book. Decide what design and style elements you like, then hire a web designer to create your own. Darren Orstman (Darren@19prince.com) did mine and I love it.

If you have time to learn, you can design your own website easily these days with WordPress or other user-friendly sites. An actor's website should be simple and easy to use. I love my website (www.jenrudin.com) because it's not cluttered and gets the information out in a clear way. Your website address should be listed on your résumé and with any additional actor profiles on sites like Actors Access or Casting Networks.

Your website should be broken into sections. Take a look at my friend Rena Strober's site (www.renastrober.com) to see her sections:

- Now appearing
- Press
- Résumé
- Photos
- Audio
- Reels
- Video

- Album

- Contact

Make sure all your links work. Just like on your résumé, make sure not to list your home address, social security number, or other personal information on your website. You don't need to watch a *Law and Order* marathon to know that we live in a scary world. Protect yourself.

AUDITION
STORIES

The Good and the Bad

I was called in to audition for the role of Chloe in Maine's Public Theatre production of *The 13th of Paris*. I was ready for regional! I had the perfect outfit and French accent (both of which I had used the previous Halloween when I randomly decided to be a French flight attendant). I had French music on my iPod to get me in the zone, and I felt emotionally prepared to play Chloe's heart-wrenching final scene. (Lost love! Tears! Suicide!) The director told me when I later got the role that she chose me because unlike the other women who had tried out, I was able to set aside jaded American notions of love. Not sure how I pulled that off, but nevertheless, SUCCESS!

And now for an epic fail: I auditioned for a casting director without having read the play from which the provided sides came. It was a comedy, but I somehow thought it was a drama and played it as such. The casting director asked me why I had wasted her time and my

When You're Asked to Self-Tape

Thanks to technology, actors now have the ability to send in self-tapes for auditions. Anyone with a decent digital camera or iPhone can tape an audition. The self-tape often replaces the in-person interview and is your first step in auditioning for a role. Virtual casting has become a very viable option for casting directors to conduct auditions and talent searches across the country and world. It's great for large searches and lets an actor in Virginia participate without having to travel. On the flip side, the competition is fierce, since everyone can compete and call themselves a professional actor. Just because you can make a beautiful audition tape does not mean you'll get the part. You still need to be a good actor. Advances in technology can't mask bad acting.

— SELF-TAPE DOS AND DON'TS —

- 👍 DO introduce yourself on camera, stating your name and hometown.

- 👍 DO memorize your lines, just as you would for an in-person audition.

- 👍 DO purchase a tripod. They're very affordable these days. (Check out the many options available on Amazon.)

- 👍 DO tape your audition against a solid-color wall or sheet, preferably not a wrinkled one, or consider purchasing a color backdrop. Check Amazon for an inexpensive color backdrop.

- 👍 DO make sure the person reading with you keeps their volume low and acting to a minimum so as not to upstage your audition.

- 👍 DO keep the pace up in your scenes. Since you are essentially directing yourself, you'll need to focus on making sure your preparation and pacing are in keeping with the script's tone.

- 👍 DO upload your audition video using a site like Hightail.com (formerly YouSendIt), Vimeo, YouTube, or Dropbox. All are easy to use and either are free or charge minimal fees.

- 👎 DON'T tape in a dark corner or in your bathroom. Make sure you have plenty of light.

- 👎 DON'T send multiple takes of each scene, unless requested by the casting office. Send your best take.

- 👎 DON'T fumble through your script. Know your lines before you tape.

There are no excuses for mediocrity, whether you're in the audition room or sending in a self-taped submission. Remember, you're a professional actor and your tape should reflect this!

AGENT'S CORNER

How has technology changed in your years as an agent?

The biggest change is self-tapes. Miley Cyrus taped several times from Tennessee for *Hannah Montana*. In the beginning we had to FedEx tapes, which cost about twenty dollars each to send. That became unviable after a while. Sending tapes via e-mail leveled the playing field. Today we spend a large part of every day taping actors at our office, or having the actor tape at home and e-mail to us. It's extended the market of where an agent can find and work with actors. You can find a great actor in Miami, Denver, or Chicago, and they don't have to move to L.A. Now people are doing tapings in their basements.

—MITCHELL GOSSETT,
senior vice president at CESD Talent Agency in New York and Los Angeles

How to Navigate Facebook and Other Social Media

I had lunch with a partner at a talent agency a few years ago. We started to chat about technology and how it's affected our business. We both lamented how our professional boundaries were challenged when we opened up our own Facebook profiles. While I griped about actors instant-messaging me on Facebook outside of regular office hours, he shared the following story about one of his clients:

One day, this particular actor updated his Facebook status to: "I FINALLY have a commercial audition after months with nothing. Glad my agents are finally working for me :)" The status came up in the agent's feed. He called the client and immediately terminated his contract. The actor was shocked. He'd meant the comment as a joke. However, the agent didn't see the status as a joke at all. He sent out an e-mail to the agency's entire client list, cautioning everyone to treat their Facebook posts professionally and cautiously.

It doesn't matter what the intent was when you tweeted or updated Facebook. It's the impact of the comment that counts. So even though this particular actor thought he was making a funny, casual status update about how happy he was to finally have an audition, the impact was far worse. He insinuated that the agency wasn't working for him. The story ended with the loss of his representation.

Last-minute voice-over auditions happen all the time, and I always make sure I have my microphone with me. I was waiting for a flight at Miami International Airport when my agent called with a last-minute voice-over audition. I ducked into the women's room and set up my microphone and laptop on the changing table in the family bathroom. I recorded the audition, but had to edit out every time someone knocked on the door and I shouted "Someone's in here!"

—JESSICA DICICCIO

–TECHNOLOGY DOS AND DON'TS–

- 👍 DO use technology to educate yourself. Subscribe to daily feeds from www.deadline.com to keep up. Visit websites like www.imdb.com, www.playbill.com, www.broadwayworld.com, www.backstage.com, and others to keep up to date on what's casting and what's in production.

- 👍 DO use your social networking sites for social networking. For instance, make a Facebook page for a play you're in. List the ticket information and other details on the page. Then invite your two thousand Facebook friends to attend.

- 👍 DO use your regular e-mail address to send a regular e-mail message (not Facebook) to invite agents, managers, and casting directors to see your work.

👍 DO use social media in positive ways to share good news: post your fantastic theater and film reviews on all your sites.

👍 DO like the official pages for Jen Rudin Casting on Facebook and other businesses. There's a reason we have separate pages for our businesses, so like as many pages as you want. I often post on the Jen Rudin Casting page what roles I'm casting, if I need audition readers, and more.

👍 DO think of your Facebook wall like the public bathroom wall in junior high school. One day in eighth grade, a friend turned on me and wrote a really mean comment about me on the bathroom wall. I'll never forget how hurt I was and how two-faced she was. The Internet is a public and scary place. Anything you post can be reposted, retweeted, and forwarded in less than one second.

👍 DO connect with other entertainment professionals on LinkedIn.

👎 DON'T stalk, instant message, or e-mail an agent, manager, or casting director on Facebook. If they've given you a business card, it will list their work e-mail. Facebook is for friends. I once got IM'd by an actor on Facebook at 6:30 A.M. Respect my privacy and I'll respect yours.

👎 DON'T post your exciting casting news on any social networking feeds until it's official and you've signed the contract. It's a good idea to ask the producer or company manager when you can officially announce your news.

👎 DON'T post photos of your bachelor party in Vegas or other "crazy" nights.

👎 DON'T post sarcastic or humorous comments about your fellow cast members. Not to sound like Mister Rogers here, but sometimes the ones we love the most are the ones we hurt the most. A comment that's funny to you can hurt someone else's feelings.

- DON'T text a casting director unless you're a close personal friend of theirs.

- DON'T be a braggart or retweet any more than necessary. My favorite actors are the ones who have other interests besides acting. Having varied interests and passions shows us that you're smart and interested in the greater world at large. So every once in a while, tweet or post an interesting article on a topic of interest. Reading the newspaper will help you to be well rounded and aware of the world, which will only make you a more interesting actor and a more informed human being!

JEN'S LAST WORD

" Use technology to connect and educate yourself but not as an excuse to disrespect professional boundaries. And power down every once in a while and treat yourself to a digital sabbatical. Remember that advances in technology and information are *not* a replacement for your own natural talent and charisma. That's still up to you. There's no app for instant talent, at least not at the time of this book's publication.

CHAPTER TEN

STAGE MOMS

HOW TO SUPPORT YOUR CHILD AND AVOID MAMA DRAMA

My mom was not a classic stage mom. Her motto to "never get excited until there's a contract to sign" kept her practical, calm, and rational throughout my entire childhood acting career. She schlepped me to auditions and lessons and used the waiting time to work on her writing projects. I only saw her get excited on a few occasions. The first was in ninth grade, when I filmed an episode of *Sesame Street*.

I'd auditioned for one role on the show and didn't get cast. But the producers liked me (and my big purple glasses) so much that they created a character for me named Jennifer with Glasses. In my episode, Luis the fix-it man finds out he needs glasses. I take him to the eye doctor, then to the optometrist's to pick out glasses. My parents were both so excited about *Sesame Street* that they argued about who would take me to the set. They compromised, and both took me. When we got to the set, they disappeared like excited kids in search of Big Bird and Oscar the Grouch. Despite my professional child actress exterior, I was inwardly geeking out too. After I dutifully filmed my scenes, I also snuck off to explore. When I found Big Bird hanging from the ceiling, I was sad at first, and then remembered that he was not actually real.

The second time I saw my mother have fun and enjoy being a "stage mom" was a few months later. I'd booked a TV movie and she accompanied me to Cincinnati for the shoot. The production offered each of us our own hotel suite, and my mother was thrilled to have such a large, quiet space to work on her novel. On the final night of the shoot, the cast and crew pulled an all-nighter filming at a mall in Florence, Kentucky. Around four thirty in the morning, I glanced over at my mother with the other moms. They were giddy and overtired, eating and smoking. At one point they were laughing so hysterically that one of the other mothers (not mine) actually fell backward in her chair. It's one of my favorite memories of my mother and me having fun on set.

My mother knew how much I loved acting and wanted to help make my dreams come true. But a professional acting career isn't like signing up to join the local soccer team. There's no set schedule for the season's games. A child can audition hundreds of times before getting cast. Parents must be prepared to spend hours driving to auditions, parking, eating, and waiting. Add in the costs of food, tolls, gas, and parking and you see that it costs a lot of money to pursue dreams. Before anything, make sure your child is really passionate about performing and that this isn't just something that you want for them.

STAGE MOMS' CORNER

What's the best advice for a child who's just starting out?

"Bloom where you're planted," advises Denise Smoker, whose daughter Marissa played Jane Banks in Disney's national tour of *Mary Poppins*. "Before you invest in classes and workshops in New York, investigate your local dance schools, vocal coaches, and community theater. If your child has an amazing experience in the Christmas show in your town, then you can consider expanding to New York, L.A., or Chicago for more training. Make sure the desire is real. Do shows close to home first so that you're not making a huge financial and travel commitment. Marissa did years of theater at Hartford Stage and the Goodspeed Opera House, near our Connecticut home. I remember when she starred in a local production of *The Secret Garden*. My husband reached over after she sang her first solo, grabbed my hand, and whispered: "She's really good! Now what?"

So Smoker researched agents for her daughter. And two years later, Marissa got cast as Jane Banks on the *Mary Poppins* tour.

Don't Become a Momager

We all know that the "stage mom" label has negative connotations. As a parent, you must try to stay calm. It's hard not to get caught up in the excitement when your child begins to audition. Be careful not to slip into the role of "momager"—mom and manager. Don't lose your perspective and become consumed with your child's career. At a certain point as your child's career progresses, I do recommend hiring a professional to be your child's manager or agent, just as I hire a professional accountant to handle my taxes. Be a parent first to your child. Your relationship with your child is far more important than any career in show business.

AUDITION STORIES

EPIC FAIL

My epic fail of an audition was for *A Christmas Story*. I forgot to present my head shot first thing to the casting director. And when he asked me how old I was, I shouted "Thirteen!" Although he told my mom how fantastic I was, this view changed instantly when he learned my age; he worried that my voice was about to change. To top it all off, on the way back to our hotel my mom slipped and fell in the dreary New York City rain. She had to get twelve stitches on her knee.

—CARL KIMBROUGH,
age fourteen

Finding an Agent or Manager for Your Child

When researching agents and managers, get referrals from friends. Look up talent agencies in your city. Check their submission policies to see what you will need to send in. It's easier for young actors than adults to get a meeting with an agent because talent agents specializing in youth are always looking for new clients. Kids grow and voices change. Yesterday's nine-year-old is tomorrow's thirteen-year-old approaching adolescence. Agents always need to keep their client files filled with smart, funny, and talented kids.

AGENT'S CORNER

What do you wish a young actor knew before they came to meet you?

Personality is key. It's really important that the child wants to do this and that the parents know that it's called show business for a reason. Parents must commit to taking their children on auditions. Even though I want the children to have fun during this process, they need to know this is a job. They need to be focused and serious, yet know when to ham it up for the camera. I wish some of the children really understood why they are here to meet me, instead of saying, "My parents told me I had to come meet you."

—BONNIE SHUMOFSKY,
Abrams Artists Agency

Audition Advice for Kids and Their Parents

I've auditioned so many children over the years, and children are either early or late for their appointment, but never on time. There's a reason we gave you an appointment time. Try to arrive ten or fifteen minutes in advance of your time. Arrive snacked and ready to go. Don't miss your appointment because you got stuck on the New Jersey Turnpike.

— AUDITION DOS AND DON'TS —

- 👍 DO have your child go over their lines ahead of time, ideally with an audition coach. If you can't meet with an audition coach, please go over the lines with them, but don't offer your own acting coaching, unless you happen to be a professional actor.

- 👍 DO have your child read out loud EVERY DAY for at least fifteen minutes. Turn off the video games and read a chapter out loud every night. I've called agents many times to tell them that their client can't read or may be dyslexic. Believe me, everyone is embarrassed. This situation can easily be avoided. If your child isn't reading out loud for fifteen minutes a day, another child somewhere else is.

- 👍 DO blow your child's nose (if necessary) before they come into the audition room. I've stopped the camera on more than one occasion and brought the parent into the audition room to take care of this.

👍 DO stop auditioning if your child's not having fun. Children may return to acting in high school or college if they rediscover their passion for it, but don't force them to continue doing something they don't want to do. It's not worth it if your child ends up resenting you!

👎 DON'T bring an entourage (or extra relatives) with you. Leave the little ones at home, as strollers can add extra chaos to an already crowded waiting room.

👎 DON'T hover near the sign-in sheet. Sign in, sit down, and wait patiently for your child's turn.

👎 DON'T make your child shake hands with us. Too many germs floating around.

👎 DON'T bring a sick child to the audition. Ask your agent if there's an alternate day to audition to avoid passing along a bug to the casting staff.

👎 DON'T linger at the audition room door trying to listen to your child's audition. Just relax in the waiting room. Remember, there's no reason to get hysterical.

Auditioning for Broadway and Tours

There are often open calls around the country for Broadway and touring shows such as *Annie, Matilda, Mary Poppins, The Lion King*, and *Billy Elliot*. You can google the shows to find out about open calls. Read the requirements carefully. Many of the shows have a height limit (usually fifty-eight inches is the cutoff) and vocal and dance requirements. Often a child will endure numerous auditions, callbacks, and group workshops before getting cast on Broadway or in a touring company. Some families relocate on their own dime to New York City for the opportunity. Others commute from the surrounding tristate area. Parents must be willing and ready to spend lots of time traveling into and out of New York City for a Broadway show.

During my time casting children for the Broadway and touring casts of *Mary Poppins*, we held three-hour "workshop" auditions for the children's roles. During the first hour, the children played specific theater games. This allowed us to observe the group—to see how they played with each other and used their imagination. We could also see which children had some type of attention deficit disorder or otherwise lacked patience and focus. The group audition atmosphere fostered a more communal audition environment and helped diminish the competitive feeling. But despite the friendly environment, everyone knew that at the end of the day, a few lucky ones would get cast and the others would either go into the files for the future or back to the soccer field.

AUDITION
STORIES

The Audition That Changed My Life

The audition that changed my life was definitely my audition for the national tour of *Lost in Yonkers*. It was an open call at Equity. I got to the audition and they announced that our monologue *had* to be from a Neil Simon play. I signed up for a time slot, then ran home and memorized a monologue from a Neil Simon play I had done a few years earlier (not from the role I had actually played). When I returned, I was surprised to find that it would be Jay Binder [a top Broadway casting director] himself personally running the audition! I booked the job and it was my first production contract, my first of many jobs booked through

Jay Binder (which later led to my Broadway debut in *The Lion King*), and the beginning of *nine* Neil Simon shows that I booked over the next three years—and the offer led to me getting my agent! All in all, quite an audition!

—TONY FREEMAN

— ASK THE —
ACTOR

What do you remember about your Mary Poppins *audition?*

I felt like I was well prepared when I went to the audition, but as I entered the waiting room where the auditions were being held that day, I remember seeing a dozen boys sitting with their parents and I started to feel a little nervous. However, the people who were watching us audition (including Thomas Schumacher, president of Disney Theatricals, and Jen Rudin!) were all extremely nice and welcoming. I went through three more auditions. A few days later my agent called. As I heard her singing a tune from *Mary Poppins*, my heart stopped. I got the role, and I made my Broadway debut at age twelve.

—ANDREW SHIPMAN,
age fifteen

Glimpses of Life on Broadway

It's a thrill for everyone in the family when a child gets cast in a Broadway show. Your child's agent will guide you through the initial details of the contract. Children are often paid a salary of around $1,700 per week. Once the agent has been paid his or her obligatory 10 percent commission and you put 15 percent away in a Coogan account,* there's not much money left at the end of the day.

Once rehearsals begin, the show's company manager† and stage manager‡ will be your point people to answer all questions. Remember that your child has been hired and contracted to perform a job. They are expected to arrive on time and act like a professional. A parent or guardian is required to pick the child up at the designated lunch break. Rehearsal days are often a relay race between parents, hired guardians, nannies, and babysitters. Rehearsals can last several weeks or months and are usually held in a Midtown studio from 10 A.M. to 6 P.M. each day, often including weekends. The production will provide a tutor to work with your child during this period.

For the Broadway company of *Mary Poppins*, we hired three sets of children to play the demanding lead roles of Jane and Michael Banks. Newly hired children often rehearsed separately from the rest of the cast, since they were replacing children who'd outgrown the role or whose contract had expired. Once they'd learned the show, the new children would have a "put-in," which is a dress rehearsal for a new cast member with the cast, crew, props, lights, and set. They would usually make their debut in the role the evening of the same day.

---

* *Coogan accounts* (a.k.a. *blocked trust accounts*) are required for child actors by the states of California, New York, Louisiana, and New Mexico. In most instances, you will have to supply proof of a trust account prior to receiving a work permit. The employer must withhold 15 percent of the minor's gross wages and deposit them into the Coogan account within fifteen days of employment. The parent must supply the Coogan account number to the employer.

† *Company managers* in a theater or a traveling company coordinate all of the traveling, accommodation, and day-to-day needs of the acting, design, and technical company members. In regional theater their job often includes renting apartments and hotel rooms, booking plane tickets, orchestrating furnishings and cleanings for rented apartments, and dealing with any special needs and requests. Company managers will also often schedule and oversee auditions and aid in contracting actors and creatives.

‡ *Stage managers* typically provide practical and organizational support to the director, actors, designers, stage crew, and technicians during the production process.

Once the show begins preview performances and then officially opens, the child's schedule shifts from rehearsals to performances. Broadway shows usually perform eight times a week. Each child in *Mary Poppins* performed their role for three or four shows a week. When not performing, the actors would be on standby offstage in case someone got sick or injured.

Some families find the performance schedule easier since the child can go back to a regular school schedule. Now your job is to bring your child to the theater at their required call time* before the performance. This is often an hour or half hour before the performance begins. Remember, your child has been hired for a job and lateness will not be tolerated.

Since parents are usually not allowed backstage in a Broadway theater, they often wait in a coffee shop, hotel bar, or diner until the show is over. On any given evening, many parents can be found congregating in the eighth-floor lounge at the Marriott Marquis hotel. One mother calls these mothers "upscale bag ladies" because of their similar rolling suitcases or backpacks. They'll be charging phones, glancing at watches, and counting down as they wait for their child's show to end so they can finally pick them up and go home.

Tips for Broadway Stage Parents

- Rent a monthly parking space if you will be driving your child to the theater every day. There are many parking lots located in the theater district. Check www.groupon.com for offers and discounts.

- If you can afford it, consider renting a studio apartment in the theater district. This option

---

* *Call time* is the time at which an individual actor is expected to be at the theater. Call times vary based on the amount of time required to do the actor's makeup and may be staggered among smaller roles to allow for dressing room space and/or makeup artists.

provides a quiet place to hang out, shower, eat, and do homework in between shows and rehearsals. It certainly beats killing time at a nearby Starbucks and can be a great option if your commute back to New Jersey, Westchester, or Connecticut is just long enough to be too long.

- Find a comfortable place to plant yourself when your child is performing their show. Many nearby hotels (Marriott Marquis and Westin) provide free wireless and comfortable lounges. You may need to order tea or a snack if you're there for extended hours.

- There are plenty of affordable places to eat, like the Westway Diner and Cafe Edison. Steer clear of the tourist traps and walk over to Ninth Avenue for some cheaper eats.

- Join an affordable gym in the area. New York Sports Club has multiple locations in the theater district.

- If you practice yoga, check out Bikram Yoga's Midtown location for classes or Yoga to the People, a donation-based studio with multiple locations throughout the city.

Films and TV Shoots

Life on a TV or film set is very different from the theater world. Call times to the set are very early, and shoots can take place in faraway locations like Australia or Canada for months at a time. Since a child under eighteen is required to have a guardian on the set with them, parents should prepare to spend long hours on the set. Bring a book, an iPad, or your knitting, and be careful not to fill up on all that free food provided by craft services.

What's your best advice for a parent accompanying their child on a film set?

Be respectful on a film set, but remember that this is a business with rules. As much as you show up and present yourself and your child as professionals, you also have to establish that you will not do everything that the crew wants, such as working longer hours than SAG allows or skipping required meal breaks. Make sure you familiarize yourself with SAG rules for minors on the set.

—MICHELE TERAN-MIZRAHI

Real-Life Stories: *Matilda* and *Mary Poppins* Mothers

Jennifer Tulchin, a stay-at-home mother from Westchester, New York, has two daughters in show business and an older son who excels in music and martial arts. When her younger daughter began rehearsals for the Broadway show *Matilda*, Jennifer often spent the entire day in the city while her daughter rehearsed. Though the Tulchins' home is just a forty-five-minute drive from the Midtown rehearsal location, unpredictable traffic made the journey difficult and she always left two hours early to be safe. During the day, while Beatrice rehearsed, it just wasn't feasible for Jennifer to drive home to start the laundry or take the dog to the groomer. Jennifer says she often feels like an ambassador or diplomat for her daughter: "You want to be useful to her and also available at a moment's notice if she needs you." Her cell phone is a permanent fixture on her belt. "I'm always on call and available to spring into action at a moment's notice," she says.

Worlds can often blur when one parent has to spend hours in the city waiting for rehearsals or the show to conclude. Thankfully for Jennifer, one of the *Matilda* moms became a certified yoga instructor and now some of the mothers attend classes in a nearby apartment while the children perform. The yoga classes have become "a life raft," Jennifer says. Time on the yoga mat is her time to think, relax, and let go of her never-ending to-do list.

Sometimes the Broadway performance schedule can be challenging for the entire family. Jen and Matt Merna's eleven-year-old son, Tyler, joined *Mary Poppins* on Broadway following his successful run as Michael Banks on the national tour. During one of Tyler's nights off from the show, Jen was just about to put her feverish four-year-old daughter to bed when the phone rang. One of the other boys who played Michael was sick and stage management needed Tyler to come into the city to stand by. It was starting to rain and Jen Merna knew it would take at least two hours for her to drive into the city. That night she felt like her life was dictated by her son's job. Tyler had a contract, so she was obligated to bring him in. Her husband was away on business and she didn't want to bring her sick daughter to a friend's house, so she put both children in the car and drove two hours in the pouring rain with a sick toddler. She dropped Tyler at the theater. The rain was so bad that it was impossible to find parking, so she stayed in the car double-parked for the two-hour show, trying her best to clean up her daughter, who'd gotten sick in the car. "It's one thing when your husband's job doesn't allow for you to take a family vacation when you want. But instead it's your child's job dictating the schedule." While nights like these were tough, the joy and amazing experiences the show brought to Tyler made it well worth the sacrifice.

When it comes to friends, school, and sports, parents face the challenge to maintain balance in their child's life. Since kids can't make the commitment to a sports team, Jen Merna makes sure that Tyler goes to soccer camps and plays lacrosse when he can. She and her husband, Matt, assure Tyler that his acting career is just one piece of his life and who he is. They often remind him that while his career is exciting, what really matters are his friends and his family.

ASK THE ACTOR

What was your audition experience like for the **Mary Poppins** *national tour?*

I met Jen Rudin when she taught a workshop in Boulder, Colorado, and she invited me to audition for the *Mary Poppins* tour. We played numerous games that tested our memory and creativity. I knew were being observed. Sometime later we moved on to singing cuts of some songs in the show. We listened politely as the others sang. The singing is always what got my stomach most twisted up, but the adrenaline and rush of the moment also fueled my eagerness. After a couple hours in the auditioning room we were let go and told we would be contacted later to be informed on if we would be called back. We were all competing for the same two spots.

I flew to New York for another round, and that audition lasted eight hours. Throughout the day kids were let go as the audition sessions progressed and there were fewer and fewer kids left. I remember kids crying when they were cut. Young actors feel the same sting of rejection that older actors do. I felt a little guilty for getting to stay, but I was also ecstatic to be getting so far. For the last part of that day, it was down to three girls and three boys, and we were switched around in pairs to sing. My final audition lasted about thirty minutes, and I got the news that I was cast as Jane Banks! I met so many talented and gracious people during my nine months with the company and it forever changed my life. If I hadn't attended that workshop in Boulder, I would never have gotten the chance to discover my dreams.

—AIDA NEITENBACH,
age seventeen

Adjusting to Tour Life

I spoke with the families of more than twenty child actors who went on tour, and their stories were united by a common thread: the strain on the siblings and parents left at home. Most tour contracts require an initial six-month commitment with a possible extension. A parent or guardian is required to travel with the child at all times. Both parent and child are provided with a weekly stipend of several hundred dollars to use for food and other living expenses. In many cases, one parent travels with the child while other family members remain at home. Marriages are often driven apart during this time. The parent on tour is faced with numerous lonely nights in a hotel room while the child performs at the theater, and this separation can take a toll on the family members left at home.

The parent is responsible for obtaining the child's school curriculum to share with the tour teachers. Parents are in charge of providing three meals a day for their children. Cooking can be a challenging task in hotels that don't provide refrigerators or microwaves. Many parents buy portable burners and frying pans, as it can be expensive to eat out every day. In many cities, parents must take a taxi to get to a Laundromat, so many will

With Abigail Droeger, Aida Neitenbach, and Christopher Flaim after a performance of Mary Poppins *during the 2009 national tour in Chicago.*
(ANGELA AYERS)

opt to do a lot of hand washing in the hotel room. Often parents try to work from the road. One father worked for six months from various hotel bathrooms so as not to disturb his sleeping son in the other room. Parents must make it clear to the children that the hotel room is their temporary home and that it's not vacation.

Dani Berger, a freelance costume designer and former Rockette, was at the gym when her daughter's manager called with an offer for the *Mary Poppins* tour. Dani felt surprise followed by joy. Then reality sank in. Her nine-year-old daughter was thrilled, but her husband Jon, a freelance musician, was initially skeptical. When the family sat down for dinner, her daughter pleaded, "Dad, what if someone gave you your dream, then took it away from you?" She convinced her father to let her accept the role and the family began to sort out the details. "Making the decision to tour or not to tour needs to be a family decision," Dani warns. "It can't be made by just one person."

Tour life is very structured for the children. They perform in the show, sleep late, and experience a one-on-one relationship with their parent that they don't get at home, especially if they have siblings. Tour life and an often-changing hotel room are hardly a vacation. When a hotel has a pool, everyone has fun. When a hotel has bedbugs, they do not.

The production travels on Monday, the technical day off. Often the flights connect through other cities and sometimes up to twelve hours can be spent in transit. Some parents I spoke to were afraid to fly and took pills to get through the turbulence. Another mother who split time on tour with a hired guardian grew to love the flights she used to fear. The flights became her treasured time alone as she sailed through the sky between her two worlds: downtime as she transitioned between the tour and her life and responsibilities back home.

Leaving Children and Spouses at Home

Shawn Senning, a Virginia-based mother of four, accompanied her son on an *Oliver* tour for nine months, leaving three children and her husband back at home. On a positive note, Shawn experienced independence for the first time in her life, since she had gotten married at a young age. But the guilt soon set in. Though Shawn tried to get home every few weeks to see her children, she felt guilty that she wasn't home to help her boys at home through their early adolescence and her daughter through her elementary school years. There were times when her husband would call her and say, "Enough. You need to come home now."

Routines

Many parents and kids settle into the structured routine of life on tour. The backdrop of the cities changes, and that dictates if their life will be easier or harder. If the hotel has a pool, the kids often do their required schooling by the pool. Many parents confide that they often feel they have to become virtually invisible to the production. And if a parent is the sole guardian, many feel lonely and desperate for adult company as they wait in their hotel rooms for the show to finish.

Parents realize quickly that tour life is not a vacation with time to sightsee or shop. Children put in many hours of rehearsal and then have to perform eight times a week, and they're expected to act like adults. Some parents indulge in backstabbing and public humiliation, anything to get their kids on top. But despite the tour hardships, all parents agree that the moment they see their children perform, they are proud and awed, and they know the sacrifices are worth it.

New Experiences on Tour

Many children's worlds expand during time on tour. Lisa Iacono's nine-year-old daughter, Jenna, saw homeless people for the first time in Detroit. "Jenna's extremely sensitive, and for her to see such desperation really brought forth an array of emotions," Lisa confided. "She felt guilty for living a dream and getting paid to perform onstage. She had me buying food for strangers, and finding homeless persons to give our leftover food to once we were moving on to a new city. Our bedtime conversations changed from all the antics onstage to things we were most thankful for and not taking blessings for granted."

Other kids see same-sex couples and affection backstage, and parents explain that some couples are "boy and boy," not always "girl and boy." Several mothers told me stories of backstage bullying and fistfights. Walking home from the show one night in Tampa, a boy who'd been bullied confided in his mother: "We just need to go home."

Hiring a Guardian for Your Child

Sometimes neither parent is available to accompany a child on tour. Ginno Murphy, a former actor in his late twenties, sold merchandise during the entire Broadway run for *Billy Elliot*. All the kids in the cast and their parents knew him, including Ben Cook, who played the Tall Boy and understudied Michael. When Ben was offered the part of Michael for the tour, Ben's parents hired Ginno to be Ben's guardian. Ginno accompanied fifteen-year-old Ben for eighteen months during Ben's run as Michael, and after three months, when Ben stepped into the role of Billy. In certain cities, Ginno and Ben were forced to share a single hotel room with two beds when a suite was not an option. This was a definite challenge for Ginno. "It's hard to share a bathroom with a fifteen-year-old. I refused to pick his wet towels up off the floor. I had to constantly remind him that I wasn't his mother or the maid." On a positive note, Ginno did get a chance to train Ben in healthy eating habits. "I always encourage Ben to choose vegetables and protein instead of candy and fast food. And believe it or not, he listens to me."

Susan Knasel chose to split time with a hired guardian when her daughter Maria toured with *Billy Elliot*. But Susan said her guilt never stopped. While on tour with Maria, she was always worried about her three sons (one severely disabled) back home in St. Louis. And then when she was home, Susan worried about her daughter's well-being with the hired guardian.

Returning Home After Tour

The transition back from life on tour is often hardest on the parents. One father spent nine months with *Mary Poppins*, and he was sure going home would be harder for his daughter than for him. He was wrong. "I'd been running things my way for nine months on the road. My wife was happy doing things her own way at home. It took us several months to get back into the groove." One mother confided: "I resented my husband when he turned out the lights at eleven P.M. I was used to the theater schedule, and going to bed after midnight. It took two years before we were back in sync with our marriage."

Despite these cautionary tales, all the time, money, guilt, sacrifices, and effort are worth it that first time parents see their child perform in front of thousands of people on Broadway or on tour. "Every little girl wants to play Jane Banks," said Barbara Rigoglioso, a New Jersey native and mother of seven, whose youngest daughter, Julianna, played the role on the *Mary Poppins* tour. "Every time I'm ready to pack up and quit the business, I see her perform onstage. It's a beautiful adventure. She loves it. I couldn't say no."

Tips for Life on Tour

- Pack lightly. Remember that you will be carrying your luggage and your child's luggage through numerous airports, on and off buses, and in and out of hotel rooms. If you pack a lot you may have to pay baggage fees at airports.

- Join airline frequent flyer programs to rack up miles. The miles can be used for a nice family vacation once the tour is over.

- Bring hand-washing laundry detergent packets in case you are staying in a hotel that's not near a convenient Laundromat.

- Consider purchasing a small electric frying pan or hot plate if you want to cook while on tour. These items can be sent in your trunk on the truck that drives the set from city to city. You can purchase these small appliances cheaply at places like Walmart, Target, or Sears.

- Stock up on nonperishables like peanut butter and tuna fish.

- Get an unlimited calling plan for your phone and check your carrier's roaming/international rates for when the tour plays cities in Canada.

- Consider getting your child a cell phone as well.

JEN'S LAST WORD

" If your child wants to perform, you must carefully consider whether or not to pursue a professional acting career. Are you (and your child) willing to put in the time, effort, and money? How do the rest of the family members feel? I've met many well-adjusted child actors who love acting and show business. I've also met many others who look back later on in life and feel they've missed out on normal kids' activities over the years because of time spent auditioning, on tour, or on set. Your child's well-being should be your number one concern when you make these big decisions.

CHAPTER ELEVEN

LOS ANGELES VS. NEW YORK

NAVIGATING FREEWAYS AND SUBWAYS

I'm twenty-one years old and auditioning again after college. One day I ask my agent if I should make the move to L.A. She shakes her head no and says, "For every seven hundred actors in New York there are seven thousand in L.A. And they're all skinner and blonder than you." And soul singer Bettye LaVette once said, "Don't show up in New York or L.A. unless they send for you." Despite this cautionary advice, every year thousands of actors move to New York or Los Angeles to pursue their dreams. Here's how to navigate the two very different meccas.

First tip: Don't waste time comparing New York to L.A. There's nothing to compare. On New York's best day, you can go to four auditions in one day and stroll through Central Park in between. On New York's worst day, the city is loud and dirty, and you're stuck in a tunnel between stations on a crowded subway. On L.A.'s best day, you're starring on a new hit TV series and driving down Ventura Boulevard in your convertible and the sky is a perfect shade of blue. On L.A.'s worst day, you're stuck in miles of traffic on the 101 freeway, late to meet an agent whom you hope will represent you.

A New York State of Mind

When pilot season ends in March, the spring college showcase season begins in New York. This is a busy few months from March through June when prominent universities invite casting directors and agents to attend their showcases featuring graduating classes in both undergraduate and graduate theater programs. I always enjoy the showcases and love seeing fresh, young, and not-yet-jaded performers. After the showcases, agents list which actors they are interested in meeting. I call spring showcase season the time when "agents stalk and casting directors shop."

After formal graduations, thousands of hopeful young actors migrate to New York City. Once they arrive, it's time to begin their professional acting careers and postgraduate lives in the city that never sleeps. Since I'm a native Manhattan gal, I'm used to the hustle and bustle and noise. But for an actor who's just gotten off the bus, the city can take some time to adjust to.

Arriving in NYC

When you first arrive in the city, buy yourself a good street map. Use the map and/or an application on your smartphone, like Google Maps, to learn your way around. Although a few TV shows shoot in studios in Brooklyn or Queens, your focus will mainly be on Manhattan for auditions and meetings. The sooner you learn the subway and bus systems, the happier (and more like a real New Yorker) you'll be.*

The Dance Belt

I was at lunch one day with actress Jennifer Cody, whom I cast as the voice of Charlotte in *The Princess and the Frog.* She was the first person who referred to the theater district area, from Forty-Second Street to Fifty-Seventh Street, as the "dance belt." This area houses many rehearsal studios (Ripley-Grier Studios, Shetler Studios), Broadway theaters, and casting and agent offices,

---

* The Metropolitan Transit Authority's website, at www.mta.info, provides maps and route information.

and is the place where actors will often spend most of their time. It's also where you will run into practically every actor you know!

Loud, Crowded, Expensive, and Smelly

On any given day, New York City can be overwhelming to one's senses. Here are some tips to handle the elements:

- **Noise:** City noise can range from everyday sirens to construction to general traffic and honking. To get any sleep in the city that never sleeps, treat yourself to some earplugs. Add an eye mask too, if you're sensitive to light. You'll quickly realize that noise in the city becomes part of your daily life. I'm often walking down the street when my phone rings. If it's an important business call and you're in the middle of hectic, loud Times Square, ducking into a nearby bank's ATM alcove is a quick way to take your phone call in "privacy."

- **Crowds:** Between tourists in Times Square, shoppers on Thirty-Fourth Street, commuters making their way toward Penn Station, and the eight million inhabitants of our great city, getting used to the crowds can take some time. Be prepared for overcrowded subways and buses, and lots of pushing. Sometimes walking through the city can feel like you're part of a school of swimming fish. Disobeying a Don't Walk sign can garner you a ticket in Pasadena, but to a New Yorker, a Don't Walk sign is merely a suggestion. New Yorkers consider jaywalking to be practically a civic duty.

- **Costs:** Rents are high, and today's affordable neighborhood is tomorrow's newest (expensive) trend. And if you don't pack your breakfast and lunch, it's easy to drop cash every day starting with your morning coffee and bagel. New Yorkers don't question a fourteen-dollar glass of wine or a twenty-dollar yoga class. After all, it costs money to live on the magical island called Manhattan.

- **Smells:** Yes, the city's stinky in the summer, when the heat, humidity, and garbage combine in one muggy stink. Sometimes the only summer breeze you feel is from an approaching subway train. Instead of sleeping with a box of frozen peas to cool your forehead on a hot summer night (yes, that's my own true story), splurge on an air conditioner. Try buying off season from a store like Bed Bath & Beyond to get a good deal, or look for used (but still functioning!) air conditioners on Craigslist.

AUDITION STORIES

The Audition That Changed My Life

The audition that changed my life and made me quake in my boots at the very same time that I felt myself slide into my soul was for a show that Jen Rudin cast. It was for the national tour of a one-woman play called *The Syringa Tree*. I was in my late twenties. I had an agent, but no clout and little self-esteem. I had been beaten down and was on the verge of giving up on my acting career. No one seemed to want me. Jen was a business colleague who had subsequently become a friend, and by some minor miracle, she called me in to audition. I was given the sides about a day and a half before. The audition material was pages and pages of one person playing multiple characters. Crazy South African dialects, native dances, the works. I got a last-minute ticket to the show the night before my audition and hid a tape recorder under my seat (sorry, Equity!). I watched in awe this tour de force in front of me, convinced that I had no business even being let into the room to read for this play. How did this actress do it?

The next day I worked on the sides, went into the audition, and I'm pretty sure words came out of my mouth. I made it past the first round, and I was sent home to do some more work. Then I made it past the second round. Was this really happening? When I got to the third round . . . something in me changed. Like, physically, in my body, in my heart, I was different. I simply now knew I could do it. I deserved to be there. The director was well known for pushing his actors, and he pushed me hard. It was terrifying and wonderful, and I ate it up with a spoon. He asked me to be human in a way I had never been asked to be anywhere before, let alone in an audition.

Somehow, in the span of those few days of auditions, I grew the beginnings of a backbone. It was the beginning of me as a grown-up.

I got that job. I worked harder than I ever have in my life. I loved and hated every minute of it. But I will never forget that audition where everything changed for me. And I will never forget Jen for giving me the opportunity to be there. You just never know where one audition will take you.

—EVA KAMINSKY

Finding a Place to Live

Don't be fooled by Jimmy and Kyle's spacious loft in the recent NBC show *Smash*. Space is tight in New York City, and rents are notoriously high. You must decide what's most important to you—light, space, location, privacy—and then learn to compromise on some of these things if the price is right. I'd suggest living with roommates, especially if you're all new to the city. Not only will your rent and utilities bills be cheaper, but you'll also have familiar company in a city that can often feel lonely. Ask friends from college to consider an apartment share.

Affordable neighborhoods to consider include Harlem, Hudson Heights, Washington Heights, and neighborhoods in Queens. Unfortunately, shows like *Girls* have made Brooklyn trendier and more expensive than ever. Unless you have a trust fund, be prepared to spend most of the money you earn at your flexible job on your monthly rent.

There are countless resources you can use to help find an apartment in New York City. You can network through friends and actors you've worked with, or scour Craigslist and Facebook for sublets. But proceed with caution.

Some of the ads on Craigslist are legitimate and posted by brokers, but many are scams. If it sounds too good to be true, it probably is. Other great online resources are StreetEasy.com and PadMapper.com, which let you search rental listings with filters like location, price, and number of bedrooms.

ASK THE REALTOR

What's your best advice for an actor looking for an apartment in New York City?

Finding a place to live in New York can be challenging. There are many Internet sites, some more reliable than others, that provide apartment listings. You can spend a *lot* of time trying to weed through countless ads for apartments (some of which do not even exist) and running around looking at apartments that you probably would not be happy living in. There's great value in working with a reputable real estate broker. A professional real estate broker will do the time-consuming apartment research and put together an appropriate tour of apartments to show you. You want your home to be clean, safe, and legal, and a good, professional broker will make that happen. When you find "the one" you want, the broker will be there from beginning to end to make sure you secure the apartment. This frees you to spend the time focusing on your career. There is a fee charged for this service, but keep in mind what's cheap is expensive. You don't want to find yourself needing to move after a short period of time because you are in a less-than-acceptable living situation or are being forced to move because of an illegal lease.

—MARCY BLOOMSTEIN,
senior vice president,
DJK Residential

Apartment-Hunting Resources in NYC

If you choose not to use a broker, here are some sites that will help you find an apartment on your own:

- Gypsy Housing, a group on Facebook. Dror Baitel, a musical director and piano player, says, "I look for my roommates on Gypsy Housing, which is relatively new. It's a group on Facebook for artists, and there are definitely a lot of actors on it. It's a great network to find apartments and shares in the city and you can save some time on the scams that come up on Craigslist. This is a pretty awesome way to get to know the people you may be sharing a place with."

- www.bangitout.com. I've used this site to find affordable sublets and studio apartments, though I still had to pay broker fees.

- www.craigslist.org

- www.urbancompass.com

- www.streeteasy.com

- www.citi-habitats.com. Actress Kate Bodenheimer says, "When I moved to the city I used Citi Habitats. A lot of their real estate

agents are also actors, so they have a great
sense of the specific needs that we actors have
when looking for apartments—like being close
to the train, affordable on our budgets, with a
lease that allows subletters, and, most
important, for us singers, friendly neighbors
and thick walls so we can practice at home!"

Food Shopping

Since you'll mostly be on foot and walking everywhere in New York City,
with no car trunk, your food shopping habits will shift. Plan to go grocery
shopping with an empty backpack or bring eco-friendly tote bags. Some
New Yorkers even carry little bags on wheels (like a small rolling suitcase)
or metal rolling carts to take to the grocery store with them, since hauling
heavy bags multiple blocks can be exhausting for those who lack upper
body strength. Prepare yourself for heightened crowds and more pushing
at the various Fairway locations around Manhattan and Brooklyn and at
the popular and often crowded Trader Joe's in Union Square, Chelsea, and
the Upper West Side. Whole Foods stores are plentiful in the city but jok-
ingly referred to as "Whole Paycheck" for a reason. Check out Fresh Direct (www.freshdirect.com), which will deliver food right to your door
(for a small delivery fee) and is a great option if you can plan to be home
during their designated delivery window or live in a building with a door-
man. Fresh Direct is also ideal for those times when you need to buy
heavier items like soda cans or things in bulk like multiple rolls of paper
towels. Local bodegas are fine for a few emergency items, but many have
cash-only policies or minimum charges to use credit cards. Though many
large supermarkets do exist in nearby New Jersey and Westchester, if you
don't have a car, these places are not a realistic option. Once you explore
your neighborhood and figure out what's close by, you'll learn what works
best for you.

JEN'S LAST WORD ON NEW YORK CITY

" Broadway does not come ringing your doorbell in Kentucky. You have to put on your comfortable city walking shoes and pound the pavement to get there. The city is your playground to pursue your dreams.

Los Angeles: You Need to Have a Plan

When I moved to L.A. in 2002, my dear friend Lori Schneide Shapiro offered to pick me up from LAX and take me to my temporary house right near the Disney lot. When I arrived at baggage claim, I was a disheveled mess: clutching duffel bags, a lunch box, two ten-pound weights, my childhood stuffed animal Boubi (the same one who'd played Sandy in my fifth-grade production of *Annie*), and way too many carry-on bags. Lori took in my chaos, then gave me wise advice that I now impart to you: "Welcome to L.A. From this moment forward, you need to have a plan."

Finding Representation in L.A.

The first step in your plan is to sort out representation. If you're thinking of going out to L.A. for pilot season or to simply test the waters, you need to line up your team of representatives. The whole point of going to L.A. is to actually get in the door to meet casting directors, and you can't get in the door without a good agent or manager to open those doors for you.

If you've already been working with an agent in New York, meet with them in person. Tell them you're considering spending time in L.A. Open up a dialogue to get their opinion. Perhaps they can recommend an agent for you to call or casting directors to meet. Some agencies have offices in both New York and Los Angeles, and the New York agent can introduce you to their L.A. colleagues. If your agency isn't bicoastal, ask if they share clients with an L.A. agency. This is a great option and the agents involved can figure out a commission spilt. I'm all about inclusivity. If you include your New York agent as part of the L.A. conversation, they'll appreciate it and advise you wisely. You certainly don't want to drop your current agent in a delusional fantasy that a big agency like CAA* will sign you when you step off the plane.

If your current agent doesn't work with any agents in L.A., consider a preliminary trip to L.A. to meet with some agents. Actors Connection and Talent Ventures Inc. have locations in L.A. so you can network with agents and managers out there. I suggest that you take your preliminary trip in the summer, when agents have more time for meetings. Of course, there's always a catch-22. An agent may not want to take a meeting if you aren't available immediately to start auditioning. Every agent will have a different opinion. Get the agent plan sorted out a few months prior to arriving. Then go out in January for pilot season with your teams in place.

Finding a Place to Live in L.A.

You get more for your money in terms of apartments in L.A., especially if you choose to live in the valley (Studio City, Burbank, Valley Village) instead

---

* *Creative Artists Agency* (CAA) is a prominent entertainment and sports agency headquartered in Los Angeles. It is well known as Hollywood's leading talent agency and it has numerous celebrity clients.

of the more expensive real estate near the Pacific Ocean in Santa Monica and Venice. "Many apartment complexes in the valley are very affordable and even come with a pool," says Stefanie Kahn, a Realtor with Bill Toth & Associates. Kahn suggests asking a parent to cosign your lease if you don't have good credit. Some challenges that are unique to L.A. apartments: parking spaces may be limited or not included with an apartment. There's more street parking in the valley neighborhoods than congested Hollywood or the more expensive Westside. Kahn cautions to tread carefully when sizing up potential roommates in L.A. "When interviewing potential roommates, try your best to pick a good one. You want to make sure your home life is stable. There's enough drama out there in the business. Actors should live in a peaceful, supportive environment. Save the drama for the stage!"

Your Car Is Your Mobile Office

When I moved to L.A., I was more afraid to drive than I was to start my new job at Disney. Over the years, I became a more experienced driver. While New Yorkers depend on public transportation every day, there are many parts of L.A. that the metro and bus systems just don't reach. If you don't drive, L.A. will definitely be a challenge.

Rent or lease a car that gets great mileage. If it's an option, choose one with a sunroof so you can get some air and see the sky when you're stuck in traffic. Your car is essentially your mobile office. You will be in this car for *hours every day*, driving to numerous auditions all over town.

Your Trunk

In New York, your purse or bag acts like a portable trunk that you carry our around with you all day. You'll need to find a good structured bag that's also somewhat stylish. One of the benefits of L.A. is that you can leave all your stuff in your car and just go to your meeting. So take advantage of your trunk. It's cleaner, classier, and more civilized to show up with just your car keys, cell phone, and audition sides then it is to haul your literal baggage into the audition room.

How to Stay Zen in Your Car

When I moved to L.A., Lori gave me her Thomas Guide, a spiral-bound street atlas. Frequently lost, I'd pull over, thumb through the Thomas Guide, and try to find what street I was on. Life is easier now that we've entered the twenty-first century and the GPS was invented. When I asked Lori for some current tips, she said: "I suggest plugging all of your appointments into your GPS *before* you start driving. If you are privileged to have a car with Bluetooth, make sure that the car and the contact numbers/GPS addresses are connected and up and running *before* you back out of your driveway. Don't forget a caddy placed in your backseat, and easy to reach, filled with water, snacks, and tissues. Finally, use your time on the road wisely. Find some podcasts or audiobooks you like to listen to, invest in satellite radio for your car, or keep your iTunes on shuffle if you just need to relax with some feel-good music."

And though many people text and read e-mails when stopped at a red light, *don't*. Practice safe and cautious driving skills.

Traffic: Meandering Your Way Through the Land of L.A.

When you look at a map, you'll see that L.A. is very spread out. There's the San Fernando Valley, which feels like a regular suburb. The valley is a great place to rent a house. You'll feel more at home and not like you're in a huge city. NBC, ABC, Universal Studios, Warner Bros., and Disney are all located in Burbank, also in the valley. When you leave the valley to drive "over the hill," you are in Hollywood and Beverly Hills. Then as you head west toward the ocean, you drive through the neighborhoods of Century City (20th Century Fox lot), Culver City (Sony lot), Westwood, Brentwood, and finally Santa Monica, Venice, and Malibu, set right next to the glorious Pacific Ocean. My friend Lori has lived in the Santa Monica area for twenty years and always says: "Why live in the valley when you can drive twenty minutes to paradise?"

Studio lots and casting offices are spread out all over L.A. It's impossible to attempt more than two or three meetings or auditions a day unless they are all in one area. I always warn people to manage their expectations. And to leave two hours ahead of your scheduled audition time to give yourself time to handle traffic and parking, especially if you have to travel from one end of the city to the other. It's hard to believe this until you spend any time in L.A. But after one day you will be shocked at the number of cars on the freeways at any given hour. It can sometimes take two hours to get from Venice to Hollywood. If you spend enough time in L.A, you'll soon discover shortcuts. Patience is not only a virtue but also a much-needed survival skill.

Everyone in L.A. thinks they're an expert on the traffic patterns. I actually think sometimes that it's easier to drive from New York to Philadelphia or another nearby city than it is to get around L.A. in a reasonable amount of time!

Parking in L.A.

When you get an audition appointment, always ask where you are supposed to park. In L.A., you need a "drive-on" to get through security at most major studios. Your name will be at security. They'll ask for identification, then advise you where to park. If you are parking on a studio lot, allow extra time, as you will often be directed to the guest area, which can be many levels down in the parking garage. If you are told to find street parking, allow yourself extra time to find a spot. Read all parking signs, as many neighborhoods in L.A. require special parking permits. I've gotten one too many tickets for parking without a permit.

Plan to arrive promptly for any audition or meeting. Anything can happen on the road—accidents, lane reductions, overturned vehicles. Better to arrive early and sit in your car in the parking garage then stress out over traffic that you can't control.

Take Fountain

Johnny Carson once asked Bette Davis for advice on the best way a starlet could get into Hollywood. Ms. Davis replied without hesitation, "Take Fountain!" (Fountain Avenue runs east to west through Hollywood, paralleling busy Sunset and Santa Monica Boulevards.)

Sushi Power Lunches

When I first moved to L.A., WME Entertainment agent Tim Curtis invited me to lunch. Since we New Yorkers are notorious for eating lunch at our desks, the lunch concept was totally foreign to me. On the day of our lunch date, I left my office in Burbank at noon, and drove to Hollywood for our 1 P.M. lunch. By the time we finished and the valet guy brought me my car, it was 2:20. I was back at my desk in Burbank at 3:00. It seemed like a huge time sink in the middle of the workday, but my colleagues assured me I'd get used to lunch. And I certainly did.

Producer Beau Flynn once told me, "When you share a meal with someone in L.A., you can do business with them for the rest of your career. Some people will become friends, and others will remain professional colleagues." Angelenos in show business love to lunch almost as much as they love to complain about the traffic. During my five years in L.A., I indulged in so much mouthwatering sushi that my mercury levels rose. Though I now must refrain from my sushi lunches, I still believe sharing a meal is one of the best ways to network in any business.

Human Contact in L.A.

In New York City, human contact is thrust upon you the moment you leave your apartment and step outside. We hustle and push onto packed subway cars, fighting every moment for personal space. L.A. is the complete opposite. You have to create your human contact. You can't just pound the pavement and knock on a casting director's door the way you can in New York City.

L.A. can often feel very lonely. It's important to have other interests and hobbies besides your acting aspirations. Perspective and balance are essential!

Holiday Weather

One can easily get seduced by L.A.'s sunny, warm weather, open blue skies, and stunning views of palm trees, ocean, and mountains. My friend the legendary director Peter Bogdanovich put it perfectly: "It's holiday weather, but no one's on holiday."

How Long to Stay in L.A.?

If you're shooting a film or a series, then you'll relocate to L.A. for a set amount of time. If you're giving pilot season a try, everyone's experience will be different. How long you decide to stay in L.A. will depend on your finances, your personal life, and if you're going on any auditions. I'm all for giving L.A. a try, but only when you are ready in all ways. It's not an easy place to navigate if you're floundering around aimlessly. You may wake up one morning and realize that a few months have gone by, all the freeways look alike, and everyone you meet wants to pitch you their screenplay. Be clear about your goals and manage your expectations. I know many actors who have relocated full time, others who are bicoastal, and some who will only show up for a specific job.

JEN'S LAST WORD ON LOS ANGELES

> - Arrange your agent meetings in advance of moving to L.A.
>
> - Become familiar with the layout of L.A. Study maps and do research.
>
> - Get a car with a GPS system and Bluetooth.
>
> - Use a broker or helpful sites like www.westsiderentals.com or www.craigslist.org to find apartments and shares.
>
> - Allow plenty of time to get to meetings and appointments.
>
> - Create a portable office in your car.

- Schedule only a few meetings per day. Unless you're flying in a helicopter, you will quickly realize how long it can take to drive just a few miles.

- Seek out community: join a book club, hiking club, yoga center, or pottery class. It's hard to make friends, so it can't hurt to find an activity that you already enjoy doing and meet new friends that way.

CHAPTER TWELVE

YOU GOT THE JOB!
NOW WHAT?

When I was a child actor and didn't get the part, my manager would usually call, especially if I'd gotten to the final round. "They're going a different way. Someone shorter, thinner, older." Or: "They didn't respond. It's not going any farther. You didn't get it." So imagine my shock and surprise when she'd call with the magic words: "You're hired! You booked the role! You're getting an offer! You got the part!" In ten seconds, all my years of hard work and talent were validated, immediately erasing the shadows of rejection poking out from beneath my sunny disposition.

After the initial excitement came the reality: details about contracts, shoot dates, and rehearsal schedules. The audition phase was over. I got the part. Now what?

Contracts and Unions

Productions work under different union contracts depending on the budget and scale of the film, TV show, or musical/play. When you get an offer for a role, your agent or the producer will go over the terms. Usually the type of contract is listed in the casting breakdown (SAG low budget, SAG scale, AEA LORT contract, etc.) so you should familiarize yourself with the pay scale *before* you audition. Arming yourself with as much knowledge as possible will save any embarrassment and surprise down the line when it comes to dates and pay rate.

Go to www.sagaftra.org or www.actorsequity.org to read about the various types of contracts offered. If you don't find the answer you're looking for, pick up the phone and call the union. You must continue to be smart and proactive, especially now that you've gotten hired for an acting job.

When Should an Actor Join the Union?

Actors often ask me whether or not they should join a union. The answer really depends on how much work you are booking. To join Actors Equity or SAG-AFTRA, there are initial union dues that can be hefty to a struggling actor. To join Actors Equity, you must pay a $1,100 initiation fee, which can be paid for over a two-year period. Basic dues at the time of this publication are $118 per year, split into two payments of $59. SAG (Screen Actors Guild) and AFTRA (American Federation of Television and Radio Actors) recently merged to form one union (SAG-AFTRA), and you can visit www.sagaftra.org to read about their membership and dues policies. If you work a certain number of hours and earn a certain amount, you can also qualify for pension and health insurance. Again, check union websites for the most current information.

I am a huge fan of unions and a proud member of the casting directors union. Remember that unions protect their workers!

Nonunion Acting Jobs

In today's market, more and more production and advertising agencies opt to hire actors for nonunion jobs. This means that the contracts and working conditions are not covered under any union contract, which saves the production money. They don't have to pay pension, health, overtime, or residuals to the actors. In these cases, the production company will likely pay actors a certain flat fee, stipend, or buyout rate for the shoot dates.

If you are going accept a nonunion job, ask as many questions as you can and make sure you're getting answers. Here are some questions to keep in mind:

- What do I need to do in order to get paid?
  Do I need to fill out a W9 and/or additional paperwork?

- What hours will I be expected to work?

- Do I bring my own clothing, or will I have a costume fitting with the wardrobe department?

You should also request a deal memo, which will detail the role, shoot dates, and performance details. Get as much as you can in writing! This will protect you later on if you need to track down payments or invoice the production company.

Earning Money

When I got my first paycheck for an acting job, my father photocopied the check, and he continued to do so over the years. Those check stubs are still in a scrapbook. They represent validation, employment, and satisfaction. If you're working with an agent or manager, the check will be mailed to their office. They'll take their proper commission (10 or 15 percent), and then cut you a new check. If you receive a check directly, it's your responsibility to pay your agent or manager (or both) their proper commission. Remember, your agent or manager spent a lot of time working for you before they earned a penny. Their commission is valuable to them. It doesn't matter if it's $60 or $6,000.

Always Act Like a Professional On Set

Now that you've got the job, you have to show up on time, organized, and ready to work. My father always reminds me to "Keep a good name." Since all you have is your name and reputation, remember that show business is a small world. Reference phone calls and e-mails are easy to make to colleagues. I'm never afraid to call a former employer and check in to see if there were any issues with an actor (or their parents) on the set or backstage. If you misbehave or do something unprofessional, trust me, someone will notice, and this can cost you a future job down the line. I want to hire the best actor for the role, but I also want to hire a professional one. Don't be stupid. Showing up late, intoxicated or hungover from the night before, or with a bad attitude is not the way to start your acting career. If you don't act like a professional, someone else is always ready and waiting in the wings to jump in and take your part.

— ASK THE —

What's your best advice for life on a TV or film set?

- The more relaxed you can be when you arrive on set, the better.

- Don't expect to get a ton of rehearsal time or private space.

- Do your warm-ups, yoga, affirmations, or whatever you need to feel present and good *before* you get to set—in your trailer/dressing room, on the subway, or in your apartment— so that you can be good to go and ready for whatever may come your way!

- Stay focused. Be totally prepared and yet completely open. Things go *fast* on a set. Be ready to "shoot the rehearsal" and to move on before you feel settled.

- Know your lines (backward and forward) and have your choices and intentions set, but be ready, willing, and able to throw that all away. Sometimes a location will change or the wardrobe will be different or any number of variables can occur where the lines change or the blocking changes.

- Be ready to go with the flow and let go of your original ideas if they're no longer serving the scene.

- Don't forget that everyone on set wants to make this project great—they all want *you* to be great.

—MADDIE CORMAN

— ASK THE —
DIRECTOR

You've just hired the actor. What's your best advice for them once they're on set?

Don't change. There are so many factors that led to you getting the part. Please don't mess with anything that may have helped. Don't cut your hair, don't shave your face. Unless the director comes up to you before the first rehearsal and gives some thoughts on your approach to the scene or the character, let that first rehearsal be as close as possible to the last read you gave in the audition. TV and film move fast, and anything you can do to make it easy on the director is a feather in your cap. Give the same performance and then let the director determine if any adjustments should be made.

Don't be afraid to make choices or contribute. Remember that first tip I gave about giving the same performance as the audition? Well, right after the first rehearsal is the time to speak up to the director about any ideas you have that may make the scene better. But it better be better, and not just different. *Don't be a director*. Let him or her figure out the scene. But, at the same time, don't be afraid to make a choice in the scene and share it with the director. They may love it, they may hate it. If you get shot down, don't take it personally. There are infinite ways to approach a scene, but at the end of the day, only one person can be the final arbiter, and it is usually the director.

Soak it up! Take in everything you see and hear, because it will only empower you to make more informed choices on the next job you get. Don't just sit in your honey wagon. Ask the PA with the walkie-talkie to take you to set so you can hang out and be a part of the company. Movies and TV are one of the last great collaborative enterprises left. Be a part of it.

—JACE ALEXANDER,
director and producer

Eight Shows a Week: Life Onstage and Off

I remember seeing a friend perform the role of Zazu in *The Lion King* on Broadway. I found him after the show to say hello. When I hugged him, he whispered: "This is so incredibly exhausting." But you have an M.F.A. from NYU, I reminded him. You're a trained actor. And isn't Broadway the dream?

Eight shows a week can be grueling for anyone. Remember that you got the part because you know how to sing, dance, and act. Now that you're onstage and living your dream, relish the thrill. And aim to keep yourself happy and healthy during the show's run and your time on and off the stage.

— ASK THE —
ACTOR

How do you maintain the vocal and physical stamina required to perform eight shows a week?

You must rest your voice as much as possible. That means no long phone conversations, complete vocal rest on your day off (depending on how vocally demanding your role is), and/or keeping quiet between shows on two-show days. Vocal rest is important and so is actual sleep, a balanced diet, and staying hydrated, all of which will keep you healthy.

Make sure you carve out the time you need to adequately warm up your instrument before each show. A full vocal and physical warm-up, in addition to the release of any tension that has inevitably crept into your shoulders, neck, back, tongue, and jaw after a day of computer use, texting, phone calls, carrying around heavy bags, etc., is *crucial* for good vocal hygiene. Figure out what works for *you*—some people meditate, roll on tennis balls or a foam roller, go to the gym, stretch, relax, do yoga, get a massage, or take a hot bath. Whatever your routine, try to keep your jaw, tongue, and neck muscles as relaxed as possible since they are all connected to your larynx. I typically incorporate parts of the Linklater voice warm-ups into my vocal and physical warm-up and then do a full singing warm-up, if the role requires it. If I am doing a role that requires a lot of belting, I would still warm up my head voice and keep it really healthy and in good shape, then I would focus on a more belt-oriented warm-up. I would also urge everyone to keep taking lessons with the teachers and coaches they trust. It's a good idea to check in every once in a while and make sure everything is in working order. In addition, while you are doing a show, keep singing other repertoire. It's good to exercise your vocal folds and sing different patterns of pitches instead of the same ones that you sing over and over, eight times a week.

One of the most tempting things to do after a show is to go out with cast mates and decompress—grab a bite and a drink. However, most places that stay open late tend to be very loud. Trying to be heard over loud music, combined with consuming an alcoholic or caffeinated beverage, can be very dehydrating and taxing on the voice. Instead, grab food to go, go home, put on a DVD, stream your favorite TV show, read, or silently "chat" with friends via Facebook, texting, or e-mail. Helpful things to keep on hand include:

- Wellness Formula, a vitamin that boosts the immune system

- Throat Coat and Breathe Easy teas or any herbal tea

- Han's Honey Loquat Syrup, a thick honey syrup that feels really soothing on the throat—good in tea or hot water

- Grether's Black Currant Pastilles to keep your mouth and throat "well oiled"—and they taste great!

—DEBORAH GRAUSMAN,
www.deborahgrausman.com

An Aha Moment: Transitioning from Acting to a Different Career

Many creative people in show business started as actors and ended up becoming agents, managers, or casting directors. Just look at some of my friends thirty years after our summers at Stagedoor Manor: Mark Saks is an award-winning casting director for *The Good Wife* and numerous other television shows; Pamela Fisher heads the youth division at Abrams Artists Agency in Los Angeles; Shawn Levy and Jeff Sharp direct and produce high-budget feature films; Steven Chaikelson is a theater producer and heads the Theater Management program at Columbia University; Amy Harris is a TV producer; and Ari Karpel's an entertainment journalist. We all use our acting skills in our current careers, and many of us would never have chosen our current career were it not for our acting journeys and the confidence and leadership skills we acquired. I know that my strong public speaking skills, assertive phone manner, and the overall discipline to get tasks done stems from my overall acting training and six summers at Stagedoor Manor undertaking difficult roles in under three weeks. During my last summer at Stagedoor, I was playing Elizabeth Bennet in *Pride and Prejudice,* and my best friend Wendy Prior was Charity in *Sweet Charity.* We stayed up late every night learning our lines. I don't think I ever worked that hard in college, which may explain why I practically failed one of my required science courses!

Just as my Stagedoor Manor friends and colleagues transitioned from acting, there may come a moment when you suddenly realize you can't or don't want to audition anymore. You may want a dog, a house, a family, and a steady job, and acting just isn't paying enough to keep the lights on. Try to visualize something else that you can do that can incorporate your acting skills and provide a steadier income. Check out www.actorsfund.org. It's a great resource for jobs, career seminars, and help with transitions.

Working in Theater

For a detailed exploration of the theater world, I'd recommend my friend and former boss Thomas Schumacher's book *How Does the Show Go On? An Introduction to the Theater.* Tom's book explains so much about producing theater and the many jobs that go on behind the scenes. Also visit www.playbill.com and scroll through their casting and jobs link. Lots of theater jobs are posted there.

Here are some jobs in the theater world:

- **Creative:** producer, director, playwright, dramaturge, composer, lyricist
- **Administrative:** artistic director, general manager, company manager, stage manager, production manager, publicist

- **Technical:** scenic designer, costume designer, lighting designer, sound designer, hair stylist, makeup artist, orchestrater, choreographer, music director

---

Becoming a Company Manager

I started out in undergrad thinking that if I went into theater, I would be an actor. I think many people think this because acting is the only job in theater that they know. I tried stage managing and suddenly the world of acting seemed so small. Why play one character in a show when you can sit in the back of a theater, call a show, and control the whole stage? Seeing an entire stage go black or hearing a roll of thunder because I called a cue was thrilling. But as much as I enjoyed stage managing, it never felt like a great fit for my skill set. I kept trying new ways to be involved in theater and eventually discovered that company management is where I belong. I'm glad that I kept myself open to new possibilities and followed where my curiosity led me, because fifteen years ago, I am not sure I even knew what a company manager did and never would have guessed that it would be where I was the happiest.

—FRED HEMMINGER,
company manager, The Lion King,
North American tour

Jobs in Film and TV

There are lots of jobs to explore in film and TV production. Check out www.mandy.com for crew jobs in your area. Here's a sampling:

- Creative: director, writer, producer
- Production: unit production manager, production coordinator, production secretary
- Art: production designer, art director
- Camera: director of photography, camera operator, loader, still photographer
- Clearances/Product placement
- Sets: set construction, set decorator
- Editorial: film editor
- Electric: gaffer, best boy electric
- Grip: key grip, best boy grip
- Locations: location manager
- Postproduction: postproduction supervisor
- Props: prop master
- Scenic
- Script supervisor
- Sound: sound mixer, sound editor, Foley artist
- Transportation: driver

— ASK THE —
PRODUCER

How did you become a film producer?

I came to New York from the small-town South to pursue a Ph.D. in literature while secretly writing fiction on the side. Upon discovering I was a lousy academic, I looked around and found that people were actually making movies in New York. This was the early nineties, in the first swell of that great wave of independent film. I got an internship on a feature film and realized that my love of storytelling combined with my ability to create efficiency and organization coupled with my willingness to work really hard made me perfectly suited to film production. I kept working and never looked back and soon found myself producing my own films. Someday soon I might even produce my own screenplay, thus bringing me full circle in this whole journey.

—JONATHAN SHOEMAKER,
Centre Street Film,
www.centrestreetfilm.com

STAGE MOMS' CORNER

Young performers may have their own aha moment and decide they want to stop auditioning. Once young performers stop having fun with the audition process, parents must pay attention. If you're dragging your child to auditions and they'd rather play lacrosse, sign them up for the team. Remember, it's their life, not yours. Whether they're starring in *Matilda* on Broadway or playing baseball, your job as a parent is to support and love your child unconditionally.

If you decide to shift gears and explore a new career option, be proactive. Take some of the advice I've given you about networking as an actor and apply it here. If you're curious to try a new career area, you have to be willing to set up informational interviews. Ask questions. Offer to intern or apprentice for free. It doesn't matter if you're twenty years old or fifty years old. Discovering a new passion is ageless!

Remember that if you stop acting, you can still enjoy the creative aspects in show business, just from a different angle. Look at my own journey from child actress to casting director. I love my life and job and I've never looked back with regrets.

— ASK A —
Savvy
STAGE MOM

How did your daughter "retire" from her acting career?

My daughter Rachel enjoyed years of auditions and bookings, but things started to shift in middle school. She didn't want to miss birthday parties or school events for auditions. She loved acting but still just wanted to be a kid. And I applauded her for that. There was one TV role that she auditioned for and got very close to booking. She was very stressed out about the fact that if she did book the role it would mean she could not perform in the school musical that she had worked so hard for. Some kids, those "serious" acting kids, would not give the school play a second thought.

The rejection issue was also a concern toward the end. At the beginning, my daughter was booking so much that rejection was not too much of a problem. And she was so young that it was not something anyone focused on. I did watch for it to become a negative, ready to pull her out at the first sign, but my daughter always seemed to have a healthy, grown-up attitude about it. It was probably harder for me, and we may never really know how the rejection part of professional acting really affected her. In some way it must have. It is a tough industry, and as she got older, the competition became tougher and the expectations of the casting directors harder to satisfy.

When the bookings really started slowing down and my daughter was about to start high school, she started losing interest in acting. Not so much the "working" part of it—just the auditioning part. It was becoming a chore. She started complaining she did not want to go to the audition. She was tired. She had too much homework. She had somewhere else to be. So, we pulled out and my daughter "retired." One part of me was relieved, and the other part was sad.

What a ride it had been. And although my daughter did all the acting and I did all the schlepping, we did it together. I do think my daughter was a bit relieved too. Maybe the pressure of feeling like she had to book something was getting to be too much. It was time to focus on something new. And acting will always be there. She knows what to do, what it takes, and people in the industry. She could go back at any time. For now, the focus is going to college and picking a major. Who knows what lies ahead?

—DANI ROGERS

JEN'S LAST WORD

" You've worked hard to get the part. Now be a professional and responsible company member onstage, on set, and behind the scenes. Remember, all you have is your name.

EPILOGUE

THE FUTURE

I'm not a prophet, but I know that our world and the entertainment industry will continue to evolve and change. Actors must be ready to embrace the future. Here are some of my predictions for how the acting world will evolve (and how you can keep up) in the next few years:

- **SOCIAL MEDIA:** There will always be new and improved versions of Twitter, Tumblr, Facebook, and Instagram. In order to be successful, you must make social media a part of your professional acting career and not just a time-wasting distraction.

- **TECHNOLOGY:** Make an effort to keep up with the changes. The world is only getting faster and faster with more devices, more apps, and constant upgrades. Still, as we all struggle to keep up, make sure you allow yourself a digital sabbatical every once in a while.

- **THE INTERNET:** More and more creative content will be filmed for the Internet.

Advertisers are putting more money into YouTube than TV. This will provide more work for actors in forms like Web series and original programming on Netflix, Amazon, Hulu, and YouTube. Get involved in this trend early by creating your own webisodes!

- **SPEED:** We are already uploading, downloading, and posting at the speed of light. As we move forward, I can only predict an even faster process of creating, submitting, and reviewing digital audition files.

- **SELF-GENERATED WORK:** Webisodes, independent films, and plays will continue to be the norm. Thanks to sites like Kickstarter and affordable camera equipment, smart and creative actors can take initiative and create their own content.

- **MORE INFORMATION AVAILABLE = MORE KNOWLEDGE = MORE PANIC:** Remember to continue to research everything you read before automatically assuming that it's the truth.

Some days, when I look into the waiting room filled with eager actors before their auditions, I see a vision of myself from thirty years ago. Technology and time have changed the backdrop, but the dreams are the same today for all actors who yearn for a life onstage, on television, or in film. And though we live in a constantly evolving digital world, there is no technology that can replace an actor's natural talent and charisma. These characteristics are timeless and intrinsic to a professional acting career.

I can't predict the future for anyone, let alone anyone's acting career. If you have a burning desire to act, then you must pursue your dream as long as you possibly can, otherwise you may have regrets later on in life. If you have an aha moment, then maybe you will redirect. Get a real estate license. Apply to law school. Train to be a yoga instructor. Adopt a dog.

Until then, pursue your dreams. Go to every audition and practice what I've preached. Be prepared. Be professional. Do your research. Leave early and bring a raincoat. Have a cup of coffee and find your personality. And always maintain your good name.

I wrote this book because I care about all of you, and I want you to succeed. Now you know all my secrets.

Life is short; enjoy the ride.

Acknowledgments

This book came to life one night over dinner with my beloved college friend Jennifer Zweben. Thank you, my dear Zweben, for offering to connect me to your mentor, Lisa Sharkey. I'm so glad we met in Sellery Hall in Madison, Wisconsin.

Thank you to Lisa Sharkey for believing in this project, taking a risk, and bringing the book to life.

This book was created under the brilliant eye of my editor, Paige Hazzan. Thank you for always keeping me on schedule and for your abundance of infectious positive energy.

Meredith Wechter and Josh Pearl at ICM connected me to my incredible agent Kari Stuart. Here's to a future filled with many more collaborations and a lifetime supply of Jo Malone candles.

Lauren Camadeco read drafts for months on end, always delivering valuable feedback with a positive spin. Lauren, I value your loyalty and admire your smarts. I will never forget that you helped me pack up my office after seven years at Disney and helped me launch Jen Rudin Casting. I am honored to serve as your mentor and to call you my friend.

The Shapiro Family (Lori, Joel, and Harel) gifted me a beautiful glass desk and created a sacred writing space in my home.

Thanks to Alan Kingsberg, my TV writing teacher, who reminded me to outline, outline, outline.

Denise Smoker read early chapters and gave me a much-needed crash course in grammar and sentence structure.

Thanks to my personal brain trust: Andy Finkelstein, Eve Rudin, Rebecka Ray, Rena Strober, Lauren Camadeco, Michael Warwick, Lori Schneide Shapiro, Wendy Prior Fentress, Ari Karpel, Bess Fifer, Gia Forakis, Jennifer Zweben, Carrie Fox, Sarah Hurwitz, Bob Marks, and Carlos Murillo.

Thank you to my parents, Jim and Marcia Rudin, for reading drafts and offering notes so quickly and so often. I will always treasure the hundreds of hours we spent together side by side, writing at the New York Society Library. You've both written many books, and your discipline and commitment inspired me to write this one.

Thank you to the New York Society Library for your peaceful fifth-floor writing room. It's one of the quietest places in the entire city, if not the entire world. I hope the very kind library staff will please forgive me for sneaking in the occasional Starbucks coffee under my hat.

Thank you to the many parents who opened up to me about their lives and their children's acting careers: Barbara Gelb, Michele Teran-Mizrahi, Emily Bauer, Barbara Rigoglioso, Barbara Safer, Dana Unger, Dani Berger, Debbie Kerner, Denise Smoker, Jeff Neitenbach, Jen Merna, Jennifer Tulchin, Linda Kimbrough, Lane Kimbrough, Lisa Iacono, Michelle Ceske, Melody de Castro, Dani Rogers, Meredith Simpson, Shawn Senning, Michelle Ackerman, Nadine Wright, Peter Kitchin, and Susan Knasel.

And finally, for all the actors whom I've met or auditioned over the years. I admire your courage. This book is for you.

Appendixes

BEST PRACTICES AND RESOURCES

Appendix A
Jen's Best Practices for Auditions

★ Prepare your audition material.

★ Make a schedule and try your best to stick to it.

★ Be a professional.

★ Respect your fellow actors in the waiting room
  and the creative teams in the audition room.

★ Listen to and follow all instructions.

★ Leave early and bring a raincoat.

★ When necessary, have a cup of coffee to help you
  find your personality.

★ It's all or nothing.

★ Bring this book with you and refer to it often!

Appendix B
Resources

Helpful Research Sites

www.imdb.com

www.ibdb.com

www.spotify.com

www.youtube.com

Casting Listings and Places to Find Audition Info

www.backstage.com

www.playbill.com

www.castingnetworks.com

www.lacasting.com

www.actorsaccess.com

www.breakdownservices.com

www.sidesexpress.com

www.realitywanted.com

www.actorsinfobooth.com

www.actorgenie.com

Publications

www.hollywoodreporter.com

www.variety.com

www.playbill.com

www.thefutoncritic.com

www.broadwayworld.com

www.ew.com

www.deadline.com

Books and Bookstores

www.dramabookshop.com

www.samuelfrench.com

www.halleonardbooks.com

Young Actors: Schools, Acting Coaches, Summer Camps and Training Programs

www.actorsconnection.com

www.aquilamorongstudio.com

www.broadwayartistsalliance.org

www.creativestudiosofatlanta.com

www.frenchwoods.com

www.margiehaber.com

www.neighborhoodplayhouse.org

www.nyfa.edu

www.oneononenyc.com

www.stagedoormanor.com

www.simoncoachinggroup.com

www.thebroadwayworkshop.com

www.tvistudios.com

www.usdan.com

Stage Parent Resources

www.bizparentz.org

www.hollywoodmomblog.com

www.showbizparentsresource.com

www.thesavvyactor.com

Actor Events and Conferences

www.actorfest.com

www.showbizexpo.com

Services and Programs for Actors

www.actorsfund.org

Photographers and Professional Head Shot Reproductions

www.amazingheadshots.com (Los Angeles)

www.douglasgorenstein.com (New York)

www.modernage.com

www.reproductions.com

Comedy and Improv

www.magnettheater.com

www.thepit-nyc.com

www.ucbtheatre.com (New York and Los Angeles)

www.secondcity.com (Chicago)

Dance Classes in New York City

www.broadwaydancecenter.com

www.stepsnyc.com

Places to Network, Attend Seminars, and Meet Agents, Managers, and Casting Directors

www.actorfest.com

www.actorsconnection.com

www.oneononenyc.com

www.thenetworknyc.com

www.tvistudios.com

Unions for Actors (U.S.)

www.actorsequity.org

www.sagaftra.org

Unions for Actors (Canada)

www.actra.ca

www.caea.com

Unions for Actors (England)

www.actorsguild.co.uk

www.equity.org.uk

Voice-Over Demo Reels and Other General VO Info

www.pdrvoicecoaching.com

www.shutupandtalk.com

www.sweetwater.com

www.voice123.com

Housing Options

www.bangitout.com (New York City)

www.citihabitats.com (New York City)

www.craigslist.com

www.streeteasy.com (New York City)

www.westsiderentals.com (Los Angeles)

Glossary of Useful Industry Terms

AGENT: An agent is a person who finds opportunities for actors, authors, film directors, musicians, models, producers, professional athletes, writers, and other people in various entertainment fields. An agent also defends, supports, and promotes the interest of his or her clients. Agents cannot produce their own shows due to conflict of interest. A talent agent must be familiar with his or her clients. An agent has to know what kind of work the client can and cannot do in order to match them with various jobs.

BUYOUT FEE: One lump-sum payment, as opposed to residuals.

CALLBACK: An invitation for a second audition or interview.

CALL TIME: The time you are due at the theater or on the set.

CASTING DIRECTOR: For major productions, the process of selecting actors for sometimes hundreds of parts requires specialized staff. A casting director, or CD, is in charge of most of the daily work involved in this process during preproduction. A casting director is sometimes assisted by a casting associate; productions with large numbers of extras may have their own extras casting director. The CD acts as a liaison between the director, the actors and their agents or managers, and the studio or network to get the characters in the script cast.

COOGAN ACCOUNT: A Coogan account (a.k.a. blocked trust account or trust account) is required by the states of California, New York, Louisiana, and New Mexico. In most instances, you will have to supply proof of a trust account prior to receiving a work permit. The employer withholds 15 percent of the minor's gross wages and deposits them into the Coogan account within fifteen days of employment. The parent must supply the Coogan account number to the employer.

HEAD SHOT: A head shot is a specific type of portrait that captures the personality inside the person.

MANAGER: A talent manager is an individual (or company) who guides the professional career of artists in the entertainment industry. The responsibility of the talent manager is to oversee the day-to-day business affairs of an artist and to advise and counsel talent concerning professional matters, long-term plans, and personal decisions that may affect their career. A manager can also help artists find an agent, or help them decide when to leave their current agent and identify who to select as a new agent. Talent agents have the authority to make deals for their clients, while managers usually can only informally establish connections with producers and studios. They do not have the ability to negotiate contracts.

MONOLOGUE: A speech presented by a single character, most often to express their thoughts out loud, though sometimes also to directly address another character or the audience.

ON HOLD: Also known as first refusal. When a producer likes you for a certain project, you get put on hold. It's a courtesy to let you know what dates to "hold" in case the producer decides to hire you.

OPEN CALL: An audition that is open to anyone who shows up (not just union actors).

PRINCIPAL ROLE: One of the main roles in a show.

RESIDUALS: Payments made to union actors each time their recorded performance is shown after the first. There are different pay scales for different types of work (TV, film, commercials) which are dictated by different contracts (low budget, made for cable, feature film, national network usage, etc.).

SIDES: Unique pages from a script to help the actor prepare for the audition. They are usually sent by the casting office to the actor or to his or her representative; sometimes they are available online at www.sidesexpress.com.

SLATE: An actor's on-camera introduction, stating their name, age (if under eighteen years old), height, and sometimes agency or hometown.

STANDBY: A performer who fills in for a cast member who has to leave in the middle of the show.

SWING: A member of the cast who understudies several chorus and/or dancing roles.